BRITISH AUTHORS

Introductory Critical Studies

JOHN KEATS

By the same author

Understanding Literature

JOHN KEATS

BY

ROBIN MAYHEAD

Senior Lecturer in English
University of Ghana

CAMBRIDGE
AT THE UNIVERSITY PRESS
1967

Published by the Syndics of the Cambridge University Press
Bentley House, 200 Euston Road, London, N.W. 1
American Branch: 32 East 57th Street, New York, N.Y. 10022

Library of Congress Catalogue Card Number: 67-10780

Printed in Great Britain
at the University Printing House, Cambridge
(Brooke Crutchley, University Printer)

GENERAL PREFACE

This study of Keats is the first in a series of short introductory critical studies of the more important British authors. The aim of the series is to go straight to the authors' works; to discuss them directly with a maximum of attention to concrete detail; to say what they are and what they do, and to indicate a valuation. The general critical attitude implied in the series is set out at some length in my *Understanding Literature*. Great literature is taken to be to a large extent self-explanatory to the reader who will attend carefully enough to what it says. 'Background' study, whether biographical or historical, is not the concern of the series.

It is hoped that this approach will suit a number of kinds of reader, in particular the general reader who would like an introduction which talks about the works themselves; and the student who would like a general critical study as a starting point, intending to go on to read more specialized works later. Since 'background' is not erected as an insuperable obstacle, readers in other English-speaking countries, countries where English is a second language, or even those for whom English is a foreign language, should find the books helpful. In Britain and the Commonwealth, students and teachers in universities and in the higher forms of secondary schools will find that the authors chosen for treatment are those most often prescribed for study in public and university examinations.

The series could be described as an attempt to make available to a wide public the results of the literary criticism of the last thirty years, and especially the methods associated with Cambridge. If the result is an increase in the reading, with enjoyment and understanding, of the great works of English literature, the books will have fulfilled their wider purpose.

R. M.

CONTENTS

CONTENTS

INTRODUCTORY

Our concern in this study will be the poems and letters of John Keats, regarded as literary works which are interesting and worthy of detailed scrutiny in themselves. There is a reason for making this rather obvious point at the start of the undertaking. For we shall be dealing with a poet who is a great literary figure in a special sense—in so special a sense, indeed, that at least as much attention has been paid by writers on Keats to the story of his life as has been given to the study of his poetry. There would not be anything very seriously wrong about this if the attention devoted to the poetry had always done it proper justice. Let it be said right away that the tale of Keats's development from his feeble poetic beginnings to the magnificent odes is one of the great stories of any kind of history, and that we cannot separate that development from the superb qualities of intelligence, the heroic determination to make a poet of himself, to which his biographers have paid justified tribute. It is hoped that some sense of those qualities will be brought home to the reader in the chapter on the letters.

To see the achievement of Keats in the context of the short but prodigiously fertile life out of which it sprang must naturally have its own fascination, and there is plenty to recommend such an approach provided that the achievement, the actual achievement in terms of literary art, really is seen. But some of Keats's most engagingly sympathetic biographers have displayed a curiously marginal kind of interest in the poems he actually wrote. There has been a tendency, both persistent and perverse, to talk more about the poetry he might have written had he lived longer!

Now this must be deplored. To put the matter as baldly as possible, Keats is a great literary figure for us today because of the words that he actually set down on paper. It is in them that he truly has his life, and those biographers, however well-intentioned, who do not treat his achieved work as the centre of their subject, are doing their hero a disservice.

Our concern, then, will be with the work itself. This does not mean that I shall pay no attention to that almost incredibly rapid development so amply celebrated by Keats's biographers, the development which makes him 'a great literary figure in a special sense'. But what we have to say about it, apart from the chapter on the letters, will be based entirely on scrutiny of the poems themselves.

Keats's work exhibits extraordinary variety, of both quality and kind. To say this is not in itself to praise him. By no means all that he wrote is 'great'. A very considerable amount—as he well knew—is not even particularly good; and some of it is downright bad. Since this book aims at increasing the number of people who understand and enjoy Keats, it is inevitable that attention should be centred on what is best in his writing. In order to define, or to help to define, that 'best', however, and to suggest the development from which the 'best' came, it will be necessary to give a certain amount of space to some of his works which are less than great. The procedure has more point in the case of Keats than it would have with most poets. No other poet in English has risen from mediocrity with such dramatic speed, and in few writers are hints of future strength so oddly entangled with much that is weakest in their earlier and inferior productions. But our object, whatever the quality of the poetry we are dealing with, will always be the same: to endeavour to see the poem in question as it really is, to determine the ways in which the poetry 'works' —or, in the case of the inferior poems, the ways in which it fails to 'work'.

The approach will be very broadly chronological, but cannot be strictly so. This is because Keats, in his short creative life, determined as he was to make himself into a poet of real worth, experimented in a number of different directions more or less simultaneously. The odes, however, strike us as the crown of his achievement, and it is for this reason that the two chapters devoted to them come after the treatment of *Lamia*, for example, although that poem was actually written later than the odes.

I preface our discussion with a glance at three extracts from poems, one from the very early work, two from Keats's maturity:

(a) For, indeed, 'tis a sweet and peculiar pleasure,
          (And blissful is he who such happiness finds,)
      To possess but a span of the hour of leisure,
          In elegant, pure, and aerial minds.   (*To Some Ladies.* 1815)

(b) She dwells with Beauty—Beauty that must die;
          And Joy, whose hand is ever at his lips
      Bidding adieu; and aching Pleasure nigh,
          Turning to poison while the bee-mouth sips:
      Ay, in the very temple of Delight
          Veil'd Melancholy has her sovran shrine,
              Though seen of none save him whose strenuous tongue
      Can burst Joy's grape against his palate fine;
          His soul shall taste the sadness of her might,
              And be among her cloudy trophies hung.
                                   (*Ode on Melancholy.* 1819)

(c)   Then saw I a wan face,
      Not pin'd by human sorrows, but bright blanch'd
      By an immortal sickness which kills not;
      It works a constant change, which happy death
      Can put no end to; deathwards progressing
      To no death was that visage; it had past
      The lily and the snow; and beyond these
      I must not think now, though I saw that face—
      But for her eyes I should have fled away.
                                   (*The Fall of Hyperion.* 1819)

We shall meet passages (b) and (c) later in this study, when they will be looked at again in the context of the poems from which they come. Meanwhile we may usefully point to one or two features that the two extracts have in common. Passage (b), which is the final stanza of one of Keats's best poems, has for its most striking characteristic a constant preoccupation with paradox. It is full of what appear to be contradictions; not so much contradictions of statement, in which one 'thing stated' is contradicted by another 'thing stated', as contradictions of feeling and association. 'Beauty', for example, is mentioned; but the word is immediately followed by the reminder that this same

Beauty must die. Beauty, which we are accustomed to thinking of as something to be contemplated and enjoyed in all its living vividness, is seen as something which must inevitably be taken away. Likewise with Joy, 'whose hand is ever at his lips *Bidding adieu*'. In the very experience of happiness is contained the recognition that it must come to an end, for it is perpetually on the brink of departure. Pleasure is there as well, but it is '*aching* Pleasure', carrying within itself the possibility of future pain, as its sweet nectar turns to 'poison'. And in the place where one would least expect to find her, 'in the very temple of *Delight*', Melancholy 'has her sovran shrine'. As a final paradox, it is only the man capable of experiencing intense happiness, the man who can experience it with the vividness of acute physical sensation, the man 'whose strenuous tongue Can burst Joy's grape against his palate fine', who can actually 'see' Melancholy herself.

In passage (*c*) the element of paradox is not so vividly apparent, but it is there nevertheless. The face is that of the Goddess Moneta, a face that is 'wan', and '*bright* blanch'd By an immortal sickness which kills not'. It is a face whose uncanny whiteness is beyond the whiteness even of 'The lily and the snow'. In this context there is a certain oddity in the word 'bright'. Its obvious function is to define the extreme and frightening whiteness of Moneta's face; it is 'bright' in the same way that the lily and the snow are 'bright'. But it is hard, if not impossible, to keep out of one's mind associations of the word 'bright' that are at odds with what strikes one as the general atmosphere of the passage. 'Bright', after all, cannot help suggesting radiance and life, both of which are opposed to 'wan' and 'deathwards progressing'.

Again, the 'sickness' by which Moneta's face is 'bright blanch'd' is described as 'an *immortal* sickness which kills not'. Admittedly the word 'sickness' need not invariably be associated with the idea of death, but to think of such an association is a more obvious thing to do than to link sickness with immortality.

The use of 'immortal', like the use of 'bright', can of course be literally explained. The word may be interpreted in two perfectly satisfactory ways, one that is quite straightforward, the other a little more subtle but still far from obscure: (1) Moneta's sickness is immortal because she eternally suffers from it; and as she cannot die, for it 'kills not', the sickness itself cannot come to an end. (2) The sickness is an immortal sickness as opposed to a mortal sickness, for a mortal sickness has the effect of bringing death to the person who suffers from it. By giving those explanations of the word, however, we do not banish the persistent impact of differing associations in the combination of 'sickness' and 'immortal'.

We can go further in our quest for paradox. Moneta's face, we are told, was 'deathwards progressing': that is to say, it gave every indication that she was journeying towards death. Yet we are then immediately informed that this progress led '*To no death*'. Death, indeed, would be for Moneta something devoutly to be wished, '*happy* death' in all truth, for it would bring to an end the sorrow of which, as we shall see later when we return to the poem, she is both the victim and the symbol. But Moneta is a Goddess, and 'happy death' can never be her lot. To be 'pin'd by *human* sorrows' would for her be enviable, since there is always an end to what is human.

Without at this point discussing the function of paradox in the two passages, we may establish one important thing. Both passages are decidedly complex, complex because our response to them as readers calls for considerable mental alertness and flexibility. In neither passage are we allowed to get away with simple acceptance of the obvious. The effect of both passages is quite disconcerting; we are made to feel uncomfortable.

> She dwells with Beauty—Beauty that must die;

That opening statement, 'She dwells with Beauty', sounds so serene, so reassuring. It is as though the melancholy with which the poem is concerned were something simple and straightforward—a trifle sad, no doubt, but with the sadness softened by the presence of beauty. Yet no sooner have we heard the statement than there comes the discomforting qualification, 'Beauty *that must die*'.

Observe that a great deal of the effect has to do with the rhythm of the words. The opening statement begins with three words of one syllable each, reaching a climax with the two syllables of the emphatically stressed word 'Beauty'. There follows a pause in the middle of the line, and then a repetition of

'Beauty', adding extra stress to the already heavy emphasis on that word. This repetition may appear to sound a note of triumph, but the remainder of the line utterly negates this impression by giving us the reverse of the pattern found in the first four words. Instead of the rise through three monosyllabic words to a climax in 'Beauty', we now have a falling sequence of three monosyllables—'that must *die*'. It is literally a 'dying fall'.

In the ensuing words there is a fine example of Keats's genius in the use of his verse-structure:

> And Joy, whose hand is ever at his lips
> Bidding adieu;

When we reach 'lips' we make a momentary pause, as well we must, for this is the end of a line. We do not know quite what is to follow, for there is not in itself anything obviously saddening in the mental picture of Joy with his hand 'ever at his lips'. But then, after the momentary suspension of the sense, come the two words sadly explaining why Joy has been thus depicted to us —'Bidding adieu'.

The great importance of rhythmic effects such as these is the contribution that they make to the meaning. They are not mere appendages to the meaning, ways of more or less gracefully dressing it up, but are part of the meaning itself. It is therefore not surprising that where we have complex meaning, we find also subtle and varied rhythm. Now, whatever may be said about passage (*a*), it cannot be asserted that its rhythm is either subtle or varied:

> For, indeed, 'tis a sweet and peculiar pleasure,
> (And blissful is he who such happiness finds,)
> To possess but a span of the hour of leisure,
> In elegant, pure, and aerial minds.

If one were asked to describe the kind of rhythmic effect made by the lines, one would probably say immediately that in them one is highly conscious of an emphatic beat:

> For, in*deed*, 'tis a *sweet* and pe*cu*liar *pleas*ure,

In other words, one is very much aware of the metrical pulse. This is because there is perfect conformity between the speech rhythm and the metre. Even if the line were part of a piece of

6

prose, one would still put the stresses quite naturally in the places assigned to them by the metre when the words are seen as part of a stanza.

Compare this with what happens in passage (*b*):

> And Joy, whose hand is ever at his lips
> Bidding adieu;

Have we the same conformity between speech rhythm and metre here? Evidently not. The metre is easily recognizable as the familiar iambic pentameter:

> And Joy, | whose hand | is e | ver at | his lips
> ⏑   —   ⏑   —   ⏑—   ⏑ —   ⏑ —

But it certainly cannot be said that the manner in which we stress the words invariably follows that pattern. In the first four words there is obvious conformity. Here speech rhythm and metre fit as exactly as they can ever be expected to fit: 'And *Joy*, whose *hand* . . .' In the last three words, however, one does not feel quite so sure. Individual readers will vary somewhat in the precise amount of stress they give to each word, but who is likely to feel that to give 'his' so light a stress as slavish conformity to the metre would dictate is altogether natural? '*At* his *lips*.' To be sure, this way of stressing the words does not make nonsense of them, as it can hardly be said to obscure their basic meaning. Yet one has an undoubted feeling of discomfort, a feeling that the words do not 'go' quite like that. It is as though 'lips' had been rather heavily underlined, with the apparent intention of making them more than usually conspicuous. The truth is that the way in which one most naturally stresses the words is to give all three approximately the same degree of weight, with a shade more emphasis on 'lips' than on the others, partly because it is the word to which those others have been leading up, and partly because it comes at the end of a line, the emphasis being imparted more by intonation than by any additional vehemence of delivery.

When we come to 'Bidding adieu', the discrepancy between speech rhythm and metre is vividly obvious:

> Bidd | ing a | dieu;
> ⏑   — ⏑   —

Can we possibly be satisfied with 'Bid*ing*'? Of course not, because we all know that the correct way to say the word is just the reverse—'*Bidd*ing'. '*A*dieu', on the other hand, fits the metrical scheme.

Now it would be absurd to maintain that *To Some Ladies* is inferior to the *Ode on Melancholy* simply because speech rhythm and metre are more at variance with one another in the latter than they are in the former. Playing off speech rhythm against metrical structure certainly often gives rise to rhythmic subtlety and variety, but it is not a virtue in itself, and a high degree of conformity between the two is not in itself a weakness. If we feel, none the less, that it *is* a weakness in the case of this stanza from *To Some Ladies*, where does the explanation lie?

In this poem Keats is setting out to pay a series of graceful compliments. Complimentary verse is not always negligible, and it so happens that a good deal of the best poetry in this genre is rhythmically exceedingly regular. The regularity can give a particular precision and *point* to the words; it can give them the neatness of well-turned compliment. The seventeenth century is rich in examples:

> I did not live until this time
> Crown'd my felicity,
> When I could say without a crime,
> I am not thine, but Thee.

(Even that apparently quite regular stanza has its moments of nonconformity, as anyone who ponders the manner in which 'Crown'd' ought to be stressed will realize.) If we hold that in some way the obviousness of the 'beat' is here a virtue, whereas in *To Some Ladies* it is a weakness, the explanation must lie in the question whether or not the obviousness of the beat in that poem is appropriate to what Keats is setting out to do. Does it, or does it not, give Keats's words the neatness of well-turned compliment?

I contend that it does not, and that the reason for this is simply that it attracts too much attention to itself. Instead of acting as a kind of 'frame' for the words, as in our seventeenth-century example, keeping them in their proper places and thus giving an effect of conciseness and precision, the metre here gives the words an obtrusively bounding gait. The metre Keats uses here, of course, is not the same as that of the seventeenth-century poem, so we do not expect it to have exactly the same kind of effect. But how can the effect that it does have be described as anything other than inappropriate? 'Ti-ti *tum* ti-ti *tum* ti-ti *tum* ti-ti *ta*-ta'—that is a crude way of representing what, in this kind of verse, is a crude rhythm. This sort of rhythm, we feel, might be all very well in a drinking-song roared by a convivial gathering of gentlemen after dinner; but in what is supposed to be a piece of delicately complimentary verse, addressed to 'elegant, pure, and aerial minds', it is out of place. There is, indeed, a woefully inept choice of means to the end. It is as though Keats, so to speak, were ignorant of the correct way to behave, not knowing the decorum proper to the occasion.

To put it differently, the lines give an impression of vulgarity. Keats is trying to sound well-bred, and doubtless for the moment he thinks he is succeeding, but his clod-hopping movements (which were plainly meant to be light and 'aerial') give him away as the unmistakable parvenu.

The gait of the words is not alone in betraying vulgarity. It is there in the very choice of language itself. 'A sweet and peculiar pleasure'; 'elegant, pure, and aerial minds'. Keats is all too conscious of being 'elegant' himself, with all the self-assurance of a youth who thinks that he knows exactly how to flatter the gentle sex in the right way. One visualizes a complacent smirk on the face of the poet, especially when he comes to '*aer*ial', which, as the culminating master-stroke of the poem, he emphasizes with what he takes to be a graceful wave of the hand.

In *To Some Ladies*, Keats is admittedly imitating the kind of bad, self-consciously 'elegant' verse in vogue at the time he began writing. No poet with the stuff of distinction in him could have remained for long under such an influence. But in Keats the development away from that sort of writing to the power and concentration of the odes and *The Fall of Hyperion* was accomplished in a mere handful of years. And it is to the poetic facts of this development that we must now turn our attention.

2

THE EARLY WORK

There is no need to devote further space to Keats's boyish attempts at delicately complimentary verse. We turn now to something equally youthful, but far more interesting:

> There the king-fisher saw his plumage bright
> Vieing with fish of brilliant dye below;
> Whose silken fins, and golden scales' light
> Cast upward, through the waves, a ruby glow:
> There saw the swan his neck of arched snow,
> And oar'd himself along with majesty;
> Sparkled his jetty eyes; his feet did show
> Beneath the waves like Afric's ebony,
> And on his back a fay reclined voluptuously.

That stanza comes from a fragment headed *Imitation of Spenser*, and it points to one of the major influences on certain aspects of Keats's poetry. Spenser, in various guises, is a continually recurring presence in his work, both early and late. Here the influence appears in the simple form of an attempt to reproduce the effect of the Spenserian stanza—the stanza of *The Faerie Queene*. The exercise is fairly successful, for Keats has managed to sound some characteristically Spenserian notes. There is the decorative effect of 'plumage bright', 'brilliant dye', 'golden scales' light', 'a ruby glow', and 'Afric's ebony', for one thing. Furthermore, the apprentice poet has caught much of the 'musical' quality of Spenser's verse, that quality which comes from Spenser's concern with making patterns out of the sounds of his words, and reducing to the smoothest minimum the rhythmic jolts and jars to which the English language is prone. This is particularly evident in the third line, where Keats is very consciously weaving patterns out of sibilants and labials:

> Whose silken fins, and golden scales' light

All this is just what one might expect from a youth who had read Spenser attentively.

Yet one is left with the odd feeling that there is something *un-*Spenserian about the stanza. And if we try to analyse this feeling, we find that it comes, not from a failure on the part of Keats to imitate his model successfully, but from the presence of positive qualities that are not Spenser's. The third line, as we have seen, is good Spenserian pastiche; but what of the transition to line four?

> Whose silken fins, and golden scales' light
> Cast upward, through the waves, a ruby glow:

Observe how Keats, by playing off the run of the sense against the verse-structure, gives a powerful thrust to the word '*upward*'. This may not be especially appropriate to the context, as one does not expect 'a ruby glow' to be flung 'upward' with the impetus of a raised fist. When one has said that, however, one has merely pointed to one of the signs of immaturity in this stanza. What is far more worth saying is that Keats, despite the inappropriateness of the device in this particular context, is already exploiting the possibilities of verse-structure. He is using his verse to enact meaning. We are not simply told that the glow was 'Cast upward'; the movement of the verse is at that point 'Cast upward' and moves through the phrase about the waves, to the glow, which arrives, so to speak, in the verse as in the imagined scene.

Again, the swan of the second half of the stanza, with his 'neck of arched snow', may recall the swans of Spenser's *Prothalamion*; but the manner in which Keats makes language enact the forward motion of the bird in line six is something that one does not normally associate with Spenser:

> And *oar'd* himself *along* with majesty;

Here the fitting of speech rhythm and metre exactly suits Keats's purpose.

Keats, then, is already aware of certain possibilities in the poetic use of language that did not particularly interest Spenser, whatever his virtues. We have to admit, however, the presence in this stanza of something else that is un-Spenserian, extremely typical of one side of Keats, but associated more with his weakness than with his strength. It is there in the last line:

> And on his back a fay *reclined voluptuously.*

If Spenser introduces us to figures who 'recline voluptuously', it is generally with the intention of casting moral disapprobation upon them. Keats, on the other hand, obviously sees the reclining fay as the most delectable feature of the whole decorative scene. Yet observe that this last line, though it is the climax of the stanza, produces a rather odd effect. With the words 'reclined voluptuously', the stanza seems almost to swoon to its close. It is as though the poet were turning away from the sharp visualization of the 'fish of brilliant dye' and the swan's 'jetty eyes', to lose himself in what, in another poem, he calls 'pleasant smotherings'.

I do not mean to suggest that the voluptuous, in poetry or elsewhere, must be shunned as morally reprehensible. Some of the most magnificent poetry in existence is gorgeously voluptuous. But voluptuousness in Keats is curiously ambiguous. The voluptuousness which he celebrates characteristically culminates in swooning, or at any rate involves a veering away from what is sharply and vividly perceived. This is well illustrated by another youthful fragment, *Calidore*:

> Young Calidore is paddling o'er the lake;
> His youthful spirit eager and awake
> To feel the beauty of a silent eve,
> Which seem'd full loath this happy world to leave;

The 'pleasant things' which Calidore sees as he paddles along are vividly and freshly brought before us. Keats is delighting in the sensuous detail of the physical world:

> Green tufted islands casting their soft shades
> Across the lake; sequester'd leafy glades,
> That through the dimness of their twilight show
> Large dock leaves, spiral foxgloves, or the glow
> Of the wild cat's eyes, or the silvery stems
> Of delicate birch trees, or long grass which hems
> A little brook.

(See once more how, in the first and second lines of that passage, Keats enacts meaning by making the sense lie literally 'Across' the verse-structure.) Calidore reaches a castle, 'gloomy, and grand', jumps ashore, and 'scarcely stays to ope the folding doors':

> Anon he leaps along the oaken floors
> Of halls and corridors.

And no sooner is he in the castle that he hears 'Delicious sounds! . . . the clang of clattering hoofs'.

From all appearances, Keats is about to treat us to another Spenserian exercise; not an exercise in imitating the Spenserian stanza, but an exercise in imitating the Spenserian atmosphere—in other words, a tale of knightly heroics in the manner of *The Faerie Queene*. The fragment which comes directly before *Calidore* in the first published volume of Keats's work begins like this:

> Lo! I must tell a tale of chivalry;
> For large white plumes are dancing in mine eye

And later on the debt to Spenser is explicitly acknowledged:

> Spenser! thy brows are arched, open, kind,
> And come like a clear sun-rise to my mind;

But *Calidore* proceeds in a distinctly odd manner. Despite the knightly presence of Sir Clerimond and Sir Gondibert, whose worth and whose fame must presumably stir young Calidore's heart to feats of emulation, he is far more preoccupied with the ladies—preoccupied with them in a very Keatsian, 'swooning' way:

> What a kiss,
> What gentle squeeze he gave each lady's hand!
> How tremblingly their delicate ancles spann'd!
> Into how sweet a trance his soul was gone,
> While whisperings of affection
> Made his delay to let their tender feet
> Come to the earth;

A few lines later, Calidore 'blesses'

> With lips that tremble, and with glistening eye
> All the soft luxury
> That nestled in his arms.

'Trance'; 'soft luxury'. Those are words of which we shall be constantly reminded as we advance through the career of Keats.

Here they are associated with what the poet plainly regards as an eminently desirable condition. Later, his attitude towards them will be equivocal and complex.

Even in *Calidore*, however, there is some hint of tension between 'luxury' on the one hand, and what may be called the 'actual' world on the other. When Calidore hears 'the kind voice of good Sir Clerimond', it comes to his ear 'like something from beyond His present being'. As his 'present being' is the state of tranced embrace in which we last saw him, he is obliged, if he is to show Sir Clerimond fitting attention, to forsake his 'present being', at any rate for a time. But he is in no great hurry about doing this:

> so he gently drew
> His warm arms, thrilling now with pulses new,
> From their sweet thrall, and forward gently bending,
> Thank'd heaven that his joy was never ending;
> While 'gainst his forehead he devoutly press'd
> A hand heaven made to succour the distress'd;
> A hand that from the world's bleak promontory
> Had lifted Calidore for deeds of glory.

The tension is not merely between Calidore's abandonment to the 'sweet thrall' and the necessity to withdraw from it; it is there also in the contrast between 'warm' and 'thrilling', which suggest something vividly physical and real, and the pervasively dreamlike atmosphere of the passage. Actual physical contact between human beings seems to be leading, paradoxically, to a condition in which the individual swoons away from what is touched and seen.

The basic tension between 'luxury' and the 'actual' is amusingly illustrated towards the end of the fragment. Calidore, who, as we have been told, is destined for 'deeds of glory',

> is burning
> To hear of knightly deeds, and gallant spurning
> Of all unworthiness;

But he is primarily interested in the tale of heroism and valour in one kind of context:

> and how the strong of arm
> Kept off dismay, and terror, and alarm
> From lovely woman:

And the thought of 'lovely woman' is so commanding that he cannot resist turning once more to the ladies actually present:

> while brimful of this
> He gave each damsel's hand so warm a kiss,
> And had such manly ardour in his eye,
> That each at other look'd half staringly;
> And then the features started into smiles
> Sweet as blue heavens o'er enchanted isles.

This time the change is from the imagination of deeds of glory to what is physically actual. Yet the last line, describing the smiles of the ladies' faces, 'Sweet as blue heavens *o'er enchanted isles*', heralds what probably would have been, if Keats had finished the poem, a return to 'trance' and 'luxury'. Why '*enchanted* isles'? The answer is that no isles, real or imaginary, are enchanted, but rather it is Calidore himself who is under the spell.

We observed in the last paragraph but one that 'Actual physical contact between human beings seems to be leading, paradoxically, to a condition in which the individual swoons away from what is touched and seen'. Is this, then, the kind of paradox which we found in our glances at passages from the *Ode on Melancholy* and *The Fall of Hyperion* in the first chapter? To that one may answer both yes and no: yes, because the kind of tension present in *Calidore* is basically of the same type as that which will constitute the very life of some of Keats's finest poetry; no, because at the stage of Keats's life when *Calidore* was written, he was not yet fully conscious of the nature of that tension. It is there already in the poetry, but he has not yet learnt to make poetry out of it.

To make poetry out of something means first of all knowing what that something is. The most interesting poetry in Keats's first volume is accordingly that in which he is exploring and defining, sometimes consciously, sometimes unawares, the different strands in his make-up. One of these we have already noted, the predilection for the voluptuous, for 'trance' and 'luxury', and we have also been made aware, in one part of *Calidore*, of that side of Keats which finds delight in the sensuous beauty of the world about him. This latter side of Keats is manifest in the sonnet *On the Grasshopper and the Cricket*:

> The poetry of earth is never dead:
>   When all the birds are faint with the hot sun,
>   And hide in cooling trees, a voice will run
> From hedge to hedge about the new-mown mead;
> That is the Grasshopper's—he takes the lead
>   In summer luxury,—he has never done
>   With his delights; for when tired out with fun
> He rests at ease beneath some pleasant weed.
> The poetry of earth is ceasing never;
>   On a lone winter evening, when the frost
>   Has wrought a silence, from the stove there shrills
> The Cricket's song, in warmth increasing ever,
>   And seems to one in drowsiness half lost,
>   The Grasshopper's among some grassy hills.

'The poetry of earth' is a theme to which Keats will constantly turn throughout his career. It is the theme, indeed, of what is perhaps his most perfect poem, the ode *To Autumn*. We should therefore consider carefully what Keats means by it. On the surface, the 'poetry of earth' might seem, in the case of this sonnet, to refer simply to the sounds made by the two insects—the 'voice' of the grasshopper, and the cricket's 'song'. Those sounds are certainly an essential part of the 'poetry of earth', but they do not account for the whole meaning of that phrase. Poetry, after all, is not, to the intelligent reader, merely a matter of sound: it is primarily a matter of organization.

The final stanza of the *Autumn* ode, as we shall see, concentrates on the 'music' of autumn, the sounds characteristic of the season. Yet it would be absurd to maintain that Keats is concerned with the 'poetry of earth' in that stanza of the poem alone. His evocations of the sights and the very feel of autumn are as much part of his response to the 'poetry of earth' as what he has to say about the sounds. It is the sense of autumn, in all its manifestations, appearing as a wonderfully harmonious whole, a superb organization in which all the parts fit, in which everything is 'right', that constitutes the 'poetry of earth' in the case of that poem. Autumn, as Keats sees it, is as highly-organized as a fine poem. Or, to put it the other way round, his ode is an attempt to render the effect of the exquisite organization of autumn in terms of highly-organized poetic language.

If we now return to the *Grasshopper and the Cricket*, we find that this poem, at a modest level, yet with genuine distinction, expresses the same sense of wholeness and organization in the natural world. The birds may be silent because of the heat of summer, but the voice of the grasshopper is there to take over the 'fun'; for it is not to be thought that in this exquisitely organized natural world the sun's heat will bring all sound and activity to a stop. Nature has made similar provision for winter. The frost may have wrought a temporary silence, but it does not last long, for the cricket is there, like the grasshopper before him, to fill the room with his 'song' and remind the person drowsing by the fireside of the voice of the grasshopper, and consequently of 'grassy hills' in summer.

The organization of the poem, which reflects the 'poetry of earth', is quite subtle. Keats uses parallels and semi-parallels to produce the effect of a harmonious whole. The birds, 'faint with the hot sun', have a semi-parallel in 'one in drowsiness half lost'; the imagined 'grassy hills' of the last line parallel the 'new-mown mead' of line four. The 'summer luxury' enjoyed by the grasshopper is a parallel to the winter luxury of 'one in drowsiness half lost', and the artificial heat of the stove is both parallel and contrast to the natural heat of the summer sun.

The reader will have noted that the word 'luxury' has a decidedly different effect here from that which it produces in *Calidore*. The winter drowsiness of the lounger by the fireside has nothing in common with 'swooning' embraces 'sweet thrall'. And the grasshopper's 'summer luxury', far from suggesting the trance-like, is described with a certain humour:

> —he takes the lead
> In summer luxury,—he has never done
> With his delights; for when tired out with fun
> He rests at ease beneath some pleasant weed.

Yet 'delights', in Keats, while often taking their source in what is very solidly real, have a habit of turning into the kind of 'luxury' we noted in *Calidore*.

To illustrate this point, let us consider the nameless poem which opens the 1817 volume. At the head of the poem, by way of epigraph, stand these words from *The Story of Rimini* by Leigh Hunt, at that time much admired by Keats: 'Places of nestling green for Poets made.' We shall see what Keats means by this epigraph in due course. The poem begins with the description of a natural scene:

> I stood tip-toe upon a little hill,
> The air was cooling, and so very still,
> That the sweet buds which with a modest pride
> Pull droopingly, in slanted curve aside,
> Their scantly leaved, and finely tapering stems,
> Had not yet lost those starry diadems
> Caught from the early sobbing of the morn
> There was wide wand'ring for the greediest eye,
> To peer about upon variety;
> Far round the horizon's crystal air to skim,
> And trace the dwindled edgings of its brim;
> I gazed awhile, and felt as light and free
> As though the fanning wings of Mercury
> Had played upon my heels:

As the last lines indicate, Keats is about to savour the 'delights' which the scene affords:

> I was light-hearted,
> And many pleasures to my vision started;
> So I straightway began to pluck a posey
> Of luxuries bright, milky, soft and rosy.

Now, these 'luxuries', of which the poet, metaphorically speaking, plucks a 'posey', are real enough, at any rate for the time being. They are culled partly from what Keats actually sees about him from the 'little hill', mostly from what the scene suggests to his imagination, or, as he puts it, his 'vision'. Yet although most of the things are imagined, the evocation of them is based upon vivid response to what has actually been seen by the poet in the past. If this is 'luxury', Keats is luxuriating in the sensuous beauty of the very concrete physical world, a sensuous beauty which, in this poem, is predominantly visual:

A bush of May flowers with the bees about them;
Ah, sure no tasteful nook would be without them;
And let a lush laburnum oversweep them,
And let long grass grow round the roots to keep them
Moist, cool and green; and shade the violets,
That they may bind the moss in leafy nets.

A filbert hedge with wildbriar overtwined,
And clumps of woodbine taking the soft wind
Upon their summer thrones; there too should be
The frequent chequer of a youngling tree,
That with a score of light green brethren shoots
From the quaint mossiness of aged roots:

We are not suggesting that this is poetry of much distinction.
'*Tasteful* nook' is no more felicitous than 'elegant, pure, and
aerial minds'. But the lines are not without hints of what will be
part of Keats's strength. In one way the flowers and foliage recall
the decorative floral imagery that we find so often in Spenser;
yet Keats does not merely decorate. We do not feel that he is
simply weaving a gorgeous tapestry out of the flowers and foliage,
but that he values them for their own characteristic quality. 'A
filbert hedge with wildbriar overtwined'—there is something
sharply seen as interesting in itself, and not merely as an item
in a decorative scheme. The very words 'A filbert hedge' are too
homely and down-to-earth to be part of a mere piece of embroidery. Again, although, as we have said, the sensuous beauty
admired by the poet is here predominantly visual, other kinds of
attractiveness are not ignored. Consider this:

And let a lush laburnum oversweep them,
And let long grass grow round the roots to keep them
Moist, cool and green;

The alliteration of the first two lines comes straight from Spenser,
though it consorts oddly with the clumsy movement of Keats's
shambling couplets. When we come to the third line, however, we
realize that something has happened, if only momentarily. Keats
has suddenly thought of using his verse-structure to some effect,
instead of remaining content with an inexpressive straggle. In

most places in this poem, as in a very great deal of the early Keats, intelligent reading of the poetry aloud involves a positive struggle against the sheer ineptitude of the verse. Run-on lines have somehow to be 'got over', with the minimum attention to verse-structure; not, as in poetry in which verse-structure is responsibly used, with a full sense of what the verse-structure does. But here we have an exception. The slight pause after 'to keep them', made necessary by the line-ending, lends a special emphasis to 'Moist', breaks the shambling gait of the verse, and makes us realize that the poet is for a moment as much concerned with the feel of the flowers as with their appearance. 'Green', in this context, is more than simply a colour, for it is associated with the moisture and the coolness which make that greenness possible.

For the time being, then, the 'luxuries' conjured up by the poet belong to the distinctly actual, physical world. This is so even when a maiden enters the scene. Keats may at this point be perilously close to abandoning himself to 'sweet thrall', but the damsel leaves him before he succumbs, and he is able to ask—with an unintentionally comic effect!—'What next?' What does come next heralds a change:

> What next? A tuft of evening primroses,
> O'er which the mind may hover till it dozes;

'Till it dozes' might, of course, betoken nothing more out of the ordinary than the drowsiness of the fireside lounger in the *Grasshopper and the Cricket*. When we link the words with what follows some sixteen lines further on, however, we realize that they have ushered in a radical shift of attention:

> For what has made the sage or poet write
> But the fair paradise of Nature's light?
> In the calm grandeur of a sober line,
> We see the waving of the mountain pine;
> And when a tale is beautifully staid,
> We feel the safety of a hawthorn glade:
> When it is moving on luxurious wings,
> The soul is lost in pleasant smotherings:

'Pleasant smotherings'—one sees to what kind of 'luxury' the poet has now been led. It is true that he immediately returns to cataloguing the sweets of the physically actual:

> Fair dewy roses brush against our faces,
> And flowering laurels spring from diamond vases;
> O'erhead we see the jasmine and sweet briar,
> And bloomy grapes laughing from green attire;

But these things, unlike earlier contributions to the 'posey', are not valued for themselves. They simply enhance the 'pleasant smotherings' in which the soul is lost. As for the next lines, they make it apparent that the virtue of this kind of state is that it affords a delicious means of escape from 'the world':

> While at our feet, the voice of crystal bubbles
> Charms us at once away from all our troubles:
> So that we feel uplifted from the world,
> Walking upon the white clouds wreath'd and curl'd.

The physically actual has now been well and truly left behind; and it is now that we realize the significance of the epigraph —'Places of nestling green for Poets made'. Such 'places' are, in Keats's view, made for poets, because they offer the poet a refuge in which he may 'nestle' away from the cares of 'the world' and give free rein to that fancy which leads him to the luxury of 'pleasant smotherings'. For Keats at this stage, the poet is one who has given himself up to such sensations, and who has from them drawn inspiration to tell such tales as those of Cupid and Psyche, Pan and Syrinx, Narcissus and Echo, Cynthia and Endymion.

In this poem, therefore, the contrast between 'luxury' and the 'actual' is associated with the nature of poetry, and the sources from which, as Keats sees it, the poet derives his power. The opposing strands in Keats's make-up, that which delights in the physically actual, and that which lapses into 'pleasant smotherings', are vividly evident to the reader, but the poet is not yet critically aware of them. The most ambitious poem in the first volume, however, entitled *Sleep and Poetry*, takes him some way in the direction of awareness. As a poem, a linguistic construction exploiting the possibilities of language within the frame of a verse-form, it is no more interesting than most of *I stood tip-toe*; yet it deserves some attention for the evidence it gives us of the directions in which Keats is subsequently to develop.

'What is more gentle than a wind in summer?' asks the poet in the first line, and the answer to that and similar questions is 'Sleep': 'Soft closer of our eyes! Low murmurer of tender lullabies!' etc. Sleep, however, does not occupy Keats for long. He soon goes on to ask, 'But what is higher beyond thought than thee?... What is it? And to what shall I compare it?' There follow some lines of vague adumbration, until finally we learn that the answer to this second set of questions is 'Poesy':

> O Poesy! for thee I hold my pen
> That am not yet a glorious denizen
> Of thy wide heaven—Should I rather kneel
> Upon some mountain-top until I feel
> A glowing spendour round about me hung,
> And echo back the voice of thine own tongue!

The conception of poetry and the poet is at first precisely what one would expect after reading *I stood tip-toe*:

> O Poesy! for thee I grasp my pen
> That am not yet a glorious denizen
> Of thy wide heaven; yet, to my ardent prayer,
> Yield from thy sanctuary some clear air,
> Smoothed for intoxication by the breath
> Of flowering bays, that I may die a death
> Of luxury,

Poetry, or 'Poesy' as Keats rather affectedly calls it, is linked with indulgence, with 'intoxication' and 'luxury'. Yet despite the abundance of sweets contemplated, it is an indulgence that has something *deathly* about it, like the swooning culmination of so much in Keats.

'O for ten years,' he exclaims, 'that I may overwhelm Myself in poesy'; and he proceeds to imagine the joys yielded by the realm 'Of Flora, and old Pan', in a semi-erotic daydream. He thinks of 'white-handed nymphs', one of them teaching 'a tame dove how it best May fan the cool air gently o'er my rest', another enchanting him by her dancing, and a third whose airs are especially seductive. What interests us more than the nymph's seductiveness, however, is the place to which she leads the poet:

> Another will entice me on, and on
> Through almond blossoms and rich cinnamon;
> Till in the bosom of a leafy world
> We rest in silence, like two gems upcurl'd
> In the recesses of a pearly shell.

Plainly this is another of those 'Places of nestling green for Poets made'. This 'leafy world' is far removed from the cares and stresses of everyday life.

But it is now that a striking change occurs. A few lines back, Keats has been saying that when he has succeeded in wooing the nymphs, 'A lovely tale of human life we'll read'. Seen in the light of what follows, this 'tale of human life' is critically dismissed as utterly inadequate, its 'loveliness' mere prettiness at best, sheer falseness at the worst:

> And can I ever bid these joys farewell?
> Yes, I must pass them for a nobler life,
> Where I may find the agonies, the strife
> Of human hearts:

And there ensues a vision, of a chariot drawn by 'steeds with streamy manes', and of 'Shapes of delight, of mystery, and fear', which may be taken to represent human life in all its variety:

> Lo! how they murmur, laugh, and smile, and weep:
> Some with upholden hand and mouth severe;
> Some with their faces muffled to the ear
> Between their arms; some, clear in youthful bloom,
> Go glad and smilingly athwart the gloom;
> Some looking back, and some with upward gaze;
> Yes, thousands in a thousand different ways
> Flit onward.

The vision passes; Keats proceeds to reflect upon what he considers to be the sorry state of poetry in the contemporary world, and then prepares himself to assume the responsibilities of the dedicated poet.

What is curious about the latter part of *Sleep and Poetry* is that although Keats tells us that he knows 'The end and aim of Poesy' he does not tell us what they are. All he can say is that

> there ever rolls
> A vast idea before me, and I glean
> Therefrom my liberty; thence, too I've seen
> The end and aim of Poesy. 'Tis clear
> As anything most true; as that the year
> Is made of the four seasons—manifest
> As a large cross, some old cathedral's crest,
> Lifted to the white clouds.

What this 'vast idea' really is, one cannot say, beyond recognizing that it has a connection with 'the agonies, the strife Of human hearts', and that Keats is not happy about associating poetry with 'pleasant smotherings'. Yet there is something odd about his attitude towards human agony and strife. When the vision of the chariot and the varied multitude has disappeared, there come some decidedly curious lines:

> The visions all are fled—the car is fled
> Into the light of heaven, and in their stead
> A sense of real things comes doubly strong,
> And, like a muddy stream, would bear along
> My soul to nothingness: but I will strive
> Against all doubtings, and will keep alive
> The thought of that same chariot, and the strange
> Journey it went.

Granted that the vision was not, in a literal sense, *real*, what it represented was surely felt by the poet to be real enough. Are 'the agonies, the strife Of human hearts' not *real*? Is it not for the sake of this reality that Keats has bidden farewell to the 'joys' of the preceding section? Yet 'real things' seem here to be despised by him; he likens them to 'a muddy stream', that would carry his soul 'to nothingness'. What is one to make of all this? Is Keats hopelessly confused?

The truth is that he is confused about the nature of 'real things'. To him the words mean simply ordinary, mundane, day-to-day existence, and he feels that the vision, though representing the human, must be something altogether more sublime than that. He is aware that 'luxury' alone cannot be the stuff of major poetry; yet at the same time he is unable to reconcile 'real things' with what he regards as the lofty status of 'Poesy'. He feels that human agony and strife ought to enter into his poetry, that he ought to be more in touch with 'human hearts' than his notion of the poetic has hitherto allowed him to be, but he has no real idea of how this is to come about. What will happen is that 'the agonies, the strife Of human hearts' will find their embodiment in his own stresses and conflicts, that these things will have a close connection with the reality of his personal existence, and that he will make major poetry out of them. At the moment, he is so confused that the attitudes he adopts towards poetry in *I stood tip-toe* and *Sleep and Poetry* are not so far distant from one another as one might at first imagine them to be.

Up to this point we have met only one genuine success among the poems, the sonnet *On the Grasshopper and the Cricket*. The 1817 volume, indeed, contains some amiable verse, but only two or three poems stand out as valuable in themselves, as opposed to the mainly diagnostic interest of the two that we have just been discussing. Of these, two are again sonnets, and it is noteworthy that both of them primarily concern Keats's experience of literature.

Sonnet IX, in which the poet describes himself walking home after an evening at the cottage of Leigh Hunt, starts with an impression of the cold night, conveyed with simplicity and precision:

> Keen, fitful gusts are whisp'ring here and there
> Among the bushes half leafless, and dry;
> The stars look very cold about the sky,
> And I have many miles on foot to fare.

The manner in which 'dry' is made to stand out at the end of line two, partly because of its position in the line, and partly because it is hard, when reading aloud, to pass intelligibly from 'leafless' to 'and dry' without an even more decided pause than the comma alone would necessarily dictate, emphasizes, with a touch of depression, that it is late autumn or early winter, and thus adds to the effect of coldness. The alliteration and heavy movement of the fourth line give an effect of weariness, which, however, is progressively dispelled by what follows:

> Yet feel I little of the cool bleak air,
>   Or of the dead leaves rustling drearily,
>   Or of those silver lamps that burn on high,
> Or of the distance from home's pleasant lair:

The rustle of the dry leaves is heard only to be disregarded; the stars are still the same stars that looked 'very cold about the sky', but the description of them now as 'silver lamps that burn on high' takes away something of their coldness. 'Silver' may still, with its suggestion of hard glitter, be associated in this context with coldness. 'Lamps' and 'burn', on the other hand, are far more suggestive of warmth. And although 'home's pleasant lair' is distant, it is the pleasantness rather than the distance of which Keats is mainly conscious, as we see from the stress 'pleasant' receives by virtue of its position in the line. Both the warmth and the pleasantness, of course, are at this moment within the poet himself, and the next lines tell us why this is so:

> For I am brimfull of the friendliness
>   That in a little cottage I have found;
> Of fair-hair'd Milton's eloquent distress,
>   And all his love for gentle Lycid drown'd;
> Of lovely Laura in her light green dress,
>   And faithful Petrarch gloriously crown'd.

It is not difficult to see what has most led to Keats's feeling of elation. He certainly values the friendship that he has found; but what has remained with him most vividly is the experience of literature, and, one conjectures, talk about literature. The triumphant culmination, 'gloriously crown'd', both reflects the mood of the poet (he is 'gloriously' elated), and contrasts most brightly with the bleakness of the sonnet's opening.

The other poem is the celebrated *On first looking into Chapman's Homer*. This has probably had rather more than its fair due of praise. It is a highly effective sonnet, but it is certainly not as close to the level of Keats's finest poetry as some commentators would suggest. The main reason for its fairly modest but undoubted success is to be found in the famous concluding line: 'Silent, upon a peak in Darien.' The effect of breathless, awe-struck silence is obtained through Keats's resourceful use of verse-structure. He is telling us of the impact made upon him by Homer in Chapman's translation:

> Then felt I like some watcher of the skies
>   When a new planet swims in to his ken;
> Or like stout Cortez when with eagle eyes
>   He star'd at the Pacific—and all his men
> Look'd at each other with a wild surmise—
>   Silent, upon a peak in Darien.

The secret is in the dramatic pause after 'wild surmise'. Three factors contribute to this: the drama of the imagined situation itself; the position of the words at the end of a line; and the fact that 'surmise' rhymes heavily with two previous words. The resulting impression is that of a wide-eyed catch of the breath, after which the isolated 'Silent' comes out with superb appropriateness. The sonnet may lack the rich concentration of Keats at his best; there is no doubt, however, that he is learning how to use verse.

I have said that it is noteworthy that both these sonnets primarily concern Keats's experience of literature. It is note-worthy because Keats, throughout his career, is aware, and ever increasingly aware, of the standards that have been set by the great literature of the past. For him these standards are intensely real. He is determined, whatever his initial shortcomings, to make himself into a genuine poet. And it is because that determination goes hand in hand with his consciousness of literary standards that he is able to write the odes, and *The Fall of Hyperion*.

3

'ENDYMION' AND THE NARRATIVE POEMS

Endymion, although the longest poem that Keats completed, is not one of his major works. This is not to deny the interest and attractiveness of much in the poem. While still using the couplets of *I stood tip-toe* and *Sleep and Poetry*, Keats moves with more sureness and even at times with subtlety. The staple of the verse, nevertheless, is immature, and therefore no amount of exegesis of the poem as an allegory of Keats's pursuit of his vocation can make any radical difference to one's estimate of it as a work of literature. Not that the 'allegorical' significance is unimportant. On the contrary, though it is probably a mistake to see *Endymion* as a consciously worked-out allegory, the under-surface meaning of some parts of the poem is of great interest, for in them we find further exploration of the tensions which we have observed to be dominating him. It is still true to say, however, that he has not yet made major poetry out of them. If the verse is immature, this is by no means simply a matter of faulty 'technique'. The immaturity of the verse is a reflection of the poet's uncertain grasp of experience. But the writing of *Endymion* was one of the ways by which he arrived at certainty of grasp and maturity of expression.

The poem is a free treatment of the Greek myth of Endymion, a chieftain king, and his passion for the Moon Goddess Cynthia. Keats has already referred to this story in *I stood tip-toe*, which was originally to have been called *Endymion*:

> He was a Poet, sure a lover too,
> Who stood on Latmus' top, what time there blew
> Soft breezes from the myrtle vale below;
> And brought in faintness solemn, sweet, and slow
> A hymn from Dian's temple; while upswelling,
> The incense went to her own starry dwelling.

> But though her face was clear as infant's eyes,
> Though she stood smiling o'er the sacrifice,
> The Poet wept at her so piteous fate,
> Wept that such beauty should be desolate:
> So in fine wrath some golden sounds he won,
> And gave meek Cynthia her Endymion.

Keats was now to assume the role of that imagined Poet of old, and in giving 'meek Cynthia her Endymion' he brought himself to the threshold of that maturity from which his finest poetry sprang.

Keats was abundantly aware of the extent and nature of the poem's shortcomings. By the time he came to write the notorious Preface to *Endymion*, he had moved far beyond them:

Knowing within myself the manner in which this Poem has been produced, it is not without a feeling of regret that I make it public.

What manner I mean, will be quite clear to the reader, who must soon perceive great inexperience, immaturity, and every error denoting a feverish attempt, rather than a deed accomplished . . .

The imagination of a boy is healthy, and the mature imagination of a man is healthy; but there is a space of life between, in which the soul is in a ferment, the character undecided, the way of life uncertain, the ambition thick-sighted: thence proceeds mawkishness . . .

Yet Keats could not have reached a critical stand of such devastating firmness without the production of *Endymion*, 'mawkishness' and all.

The mawkishness of the poem, though not perhaps so damaging as Keats felt when he wrote the Preface, is a manifestation of that weakness against which we found him struggling, with incomplete success, in *Sleep and Poetry*. It is connected with the predilection for 'luxury' and all that we have found to be associated with that word. If not at this point especially obvious or offensive, the note of mawkishness is sounded in the famous opening lines of *Endymion*:

> A thing of beauty is a joy for ever:
> Its loveliness increases; it will never
> Pass into nothingness; but still will keep
> A bower quiet for us, and a sleep
> Full of sweet dreams, and health, and quiet breathing.

'A bower quiet for us': that is strongly reminiscent of one of those 'Places of nestling green for Poets made'. 'Sweet dreams' intensifies the impression that what Keats takes to be the supreme virtue of 'A thing of beauty' is its power to lead us away from the cares of the world. 'A thing of beauty' is thus primarily an invitation to a daydream. The poet seems to have forgotten all about 'the agonies, the strife Of human hearts'. Yet there is something in the lines which unobtrusively, but none the less definitely, counteracts the overall impression that they produce. If we try to locate it, we find that this un-mawkish note is to be heard in the fifth line: 'Full of sweet dreams, and health, and quiet breathing.'

Now, if there is one word that we would not think of associating with the cult of 'luxury', it is the word 'health'. Indeed, as we have remarked, there is something deathly, and thus exceedingly unhealthy, in Keats's abandonment to the thought of unbridled sensuous indulgence. Dying a death of luxury, and contemplating the joys of a 'bower' sealed against worldly care, are part of the same early Keatsian appetite. And yet there is this paradoxical word 'health'. What is it doing there?

The only answer one can make is that the word's presence is paradoxical, and that here we have a foretaste of the very quality we diagnosed when we looked at two pieces of mature Keats in our first chapter. No doubt one might frame some explanation of the word's appearance which would bring it into line with the general feeling of the passage. One could say, for instance, that for Keats it is refuge in sweet dreams that brings health, and that it is drab reality which is unhealthy. The succeeding lines would seem to justify that interpretation:

> Therefore, on every morrow, are we wreathing
> A flowery band to bind us to the earth,
> Spite of despondence, of the inhuman dearth
> Of noble natures, of the gloomy days,
> Of all the unhealthy and o'er-darkened ways
> Made for our searching: yes, in spite of all,
> Some shape of beauty moves away the pall
> From our dark spirits.

'The unhealthy and o'er-darkened ways' are things from which beauty affords a refuge. It would appear, then, that Keats links health with a conception of beauty which strikes one as being rather the reverse of healthy.

Yet can such an interpretation be accepted simply, without further comment? If we answer that it cannot, it is because of the language Keats uses. Part of his meaning lies in that interpretation, but only part; and it is the other part of the total significance that foreshadows the great poetry to come. Consider, for example, 'A flowery band to bind us to the earth'. The words 'A flowery band' suggest the kind of sweet fancy with which Keats diverts himself in *I stood tip-toe*. But it is the function of this sweet fancy *to bind us to the earth*. Surely being bound to the earth implies the clear opposite of escape into a luxurious cloud-cuckoo land? The poet may, of course, mean by the word 'earth' nothing more than the ideally sweet landscape in which we have already so often found his imagination roving. If that is so, being bound to the earth is merely one of the ingredients of a life of 'luxury'. Yet, even if Keats thought at the time of writing the lines that his meaning went no further than that, the reader cannot keep out of his mind quite other possibilities. Perhaps Keats did not consciously intend this to be so. The overall effect of *Endymion* would suggest that he probably did not. But the fact remains that 'to bind us to the earth' has inescapable implications of being rooted in the firm, the solid.

It is the same with 'the unhealthy and o'er-darkened ways'. Keats may wish to turn away from them and contemplate nothing but what is beautiful, yet the words 'Made *for our searching*' suggest, if only indirectly, that he knows this to be impossible. They imply neither a horrified shunning of the unpleasant things in life, nor a passive acceptance of them, but rather an active, positive effort to explore them. Once again, Keats may be consciously saying no more than that although unpleasant things are, or seem to be, '*Made* for our searching', we shall do well to resist the invitation to carry out the search, and turn instead to things of beauty. And yet, even if that was the whole of the poet's conscious meaning, the reader cannot escape from the other quite different interpretation.

These paradoxes affect our view of the word 'health'. In this context, as we have observed, 'sweet dreams' and 'health' may appear to be offered by Keats as belonging to the same family. Yet 'health' obstinately resists such a classification. Like 'to bind us to the earth' and 'Made for our searching', the word cannot help suggesting something much more positive. Seen in this light, the immediate context of the word becomes more interesting than one might have supposed. A thing of beauty, we are told,

> will keep
> A bower quiet for us, and a sleep
> Full of sweet dreams, and health, and quiet breathing.

The 'bower' needs no more comment than we have already given it. The 'sleep', however, invites further examination. Keats is using the word figuratively, for he is not referring to physical sleep but rather to a state of mind induced by the contemplation of the beautiful. As we observed, 'A thing of beauty' is regarded here as primarily an invitation to a daydream. But although the use of the word is figurative, the literal associations of physical sleep cannot be excluded. And if the 'sweet dreams' may be written off as merely mawkish, 'health, and quiet breathing' cannot be dismissed in that way. What they suggest is something truly life-bringing, a healthful slumber into which there intrudes nothing of the feverish or troubled. It is a very different thing from the sweet trance of Calidore. We thus have the curious situation of seeing an approach to beauty which recalls the unsatisfactory note of much that we have already come across in Keats, expressed in language whose associations seem, as it were, to 'kick' against the prevalent feeling.

What is really happening is that Keats is moving towards a more adequate view of both beauty in particular and life in general. It is this which explains the paradoxes we have noted in the introductory lines of *Endymion*, paradoxes which convey the impression of a vigorous mind resisting, perhaps unconsciously, a set of views to which it is apparently committed. I say '*perhaps* unconsciously', for it is unwise and unprofitable to speculate at all closely on distinctions between the conscious and the unconscious in an artist's work. The only thing that really matters is the work he has produced. In the case of *Endymion*, the overall effect of the work that Keats has produced suggests that he was not, on the whole, what we normally call 'conscious' of resisting unsatisfactory points of view that he was fast growing out of. One feels that if he had been fully aware of these urges to resist, he would have written a different kind of poem. Interesting paradoxes merely hint at a richer and more complex poetry than that of *Endymion*; they are not yet an integral part of the artistic structure. What we can say with perfect certainty is that Keats was well aware of what he had to resist by the time he came to write the Preface.

The verse of *Endymion* may conveniently be illustrated, both at its very best and at its staple level, in the following passage, which comes soon after the opening:

> Upon the sides of Latmos was outspread
> A mighty forest; for the moist earth fed
> So plenteously all weed-hidden roots
> Into o'er-hanging boughs, and precious fruits.
> And it had gloomy shades, sequestered deep,
> Where no man went; and if from shepherd's keep
> A lamb strayed far a-down those inmost glens,
> Never again saw he the happy pens
> Whither his brethren, bleating with content,
> Over the hills at every nightfall went.

In the second, third, and fourth lines there is a foretaste of the way in which Keats will handle language in the *Autumn* ode. To articulate clearly, when reading aloud, 'the moist earth fed So plenteously all weed-hidden roots', demands a certain effort, owing to the thickly clustering consonants which have to be carefully detached from one another if the words are to sound properly intelligible. The effect of heaviness produced by the effort of articulation suggests the weight and therefore the abundance of the 'precious fruits' growing on the 'o'er-hanging boughs'. This enactment of meaning by the movement of the language points forward to the similar effect of 'To bend with apples the moss'd cottage-trees', in *To Autumn*. One may go further, and see in the clustered consonants of 'weed-hidden roots' a suggestion of the tightly-embedded roots themselves, and also the thickness of the weeds growing over them. Again there is an analogy in a mature poem—'Wolf's-bane, tight-rooted', in the *Ode on Melancholy*.

There are a good many effects of this kind in *Endymion*, and they show how strikingly Keats's grasp of the possibilities of language is developing. The general level, however, is indicated by the lines beginning 'And it had gloomy shades'. This is verse of fairly respectable efficiency, but of no rhythmic interest, and informed by no sense of pressure and richness in the language. It is precisely the kind of verse that one would expect to go with the thin pastoral fare of lambs and shepherds, with all their 'pretty' literary associations.

The word 'pretty' sums up the effect of most of the poem. It has a prettiness derived from the pastoral poetry of the sixteenth and seventeenth centuries. The narrative admittedly strays far from its initial pastoral setting, but behind it lie Spenser's *Shepheard's Calendar* and the minor pastoral poems of Milton, as we can see from the passage leading up to the first appearance of Endymion himself:

> Leading the way, young damsels danced along,
> Bearing the burden of a shepherd song;
> Each having a white wicker over brimmed
> With April's tender younglings: next, well trimm'd,
> A crowd of shepherds with as sunburnt looks
> As may be read of in Arcadian books;

Endymion enters the scene, and we are soon told that his smiling countenance is deceptive, for the observant onlooker can discern 'A lurking trouble in his nether lip'. Later on his unhappiness becomes obvious to all:

> Now indeed
> His senses had swoon'd off: he did not heed
> The sudden silence, or the whispers low,
> Or the old eyes dissolving at his woe,
> Or anxious calls, or close of trembling palms,
> Or maiden's sigh, that grief itself embalms;
> But in the self-same fixed trance he kept,
> Like one who on the earth had never stept.

'Swoon'd' and 'trance', of course, remind us of a poetic manner by now familiar. It is worth pointing out, however, that this condition in which Endymion finds himself, unlike Calidore's sweet trance, is not portrayed by the poet as in itself a desirable or enviable state. If this is 'luxury', it is luxury of a peculiarly bitter kind.

We are to discover, none the less, that Endymion's woe springs from the sorrowful recollection of an ecstatic experience, as he tells his sister Peona the story of his dream-vision of Cynthia. Yet it is more than what one usually means by a vision, for it brings Cynthia and Endymion into actual physical contact. At first the description of this is couched in familiar Keatsian terms:

> She took an airy range,
> And then, towards me, like a very maid,
> Came blushing, waning, willing, and afraid,
> And press'd me by the hand: Ah! 'twas too much;
> Methought I fainted at the charmed touch,

But what follows ten lines further on, though plainly related to this, is rather different in its total effect:

> Soon, as it seem'd, we left our journeying high,
> And straightway into frightful eddies swoop'd:
> Such as aye muster where grey time has scoop'd
> Huge dens and caverns in a mountain's side:
> There hollow sounds arous'd me, and I sigh'd
> To faint once more by looking at my bliss—
> I was distracted; madly did I kiss
> The wooing arms which held me, and did give
> My eyes at once to death: but 'twas to live,
> To take in draughts of life from the gold fount
> Of kind and passionate looks; to count and count
> The moments, by some greedy help that seem'd
> A second self, that each might be redeem'd
> And plunder'd of its load of blessedness.

The first thing that we notice here, reading the passage in the light of our previous experience of Keats, is the contrast between the expectation of death, and the 'draughts of life'. Endymion anticipates death, partly because of the 'frightful eddies' and threatening 'hollow sounds', and partly because he obviously

desires it. Death, in the arms of his goddess, is the blessed consummation to which his frenzied kisses are leading. All this is in
line with what we have described as the deathly side of Keats's
cult of 'luxury'. But Endymion, while giving his eyes 'at once to
death', paradoxically meets life, an upsurging life suggested by
the rhythm. Note the effect produced by the stresses on '*live*',
'*draughts* of *life*', '*count* and *count*'. The 'life' that Endymion
finds in the arms of Cynthia is in itself a kind of indulgence, as
the word 'greedy' tells us; yet the passage as a whole gives
evidence of a growing complexity of feeling in Keats, a complexity
which affects his treatment of the very idea of indulgence. Indulgence may still have something morbid and 'luxurious' about it,
but that is by no means the whole story. Keats now evokes feelings
of a different kind, which at the same time are placed in close
juxtaposition with Endymion's willing abandonment to death. The
poet is paving the way for his subtle and highly concentrated
treatment of the theme of indulgence in the *Ode on Melancholy*.

There is a hint of the later concentration in the last line of this
passage, 'And plunder'd of its load of blessedness'. The basic
meaning is clear, as far as the effect of the words as statement is
concerned: Endymion wishes to savour the bliss of every moment
to the absolute full. But that does not take into account the effect
of the words as suggestion. Looked at from this point of view,
the combination of words is rather unusual. The idea of plunder-
ing a load is familiar enough, and is especially acceptable here,
since '*gold* fount' links up with the words to make the load appear
metaphorically to be a load of treasure. 'Blessedness', however,
though it is easy to think of as a treasure, arouses associations
which conflict with those evoked by 'plunder'd'. 'Blessedness'
suggests serenity and even sanctity; whereas 'plunder'd' carries
associations of wrong-doing and guilt, desperation, and even
violence.

The disparate associations conjured up by the language reflect
the complex emotion of Endymion, as he clutches at his joy with
a feeling of desperation born out of the fear that it must soon pass,
and also with a guilty sense that it is a happiness which he ought
not, as a human, to be enjoying.

The happiness does indeed pass; the visionary experience comes to an end, and Endymion finishes his story. Peona tries to rally his spirits by reproaching him for pining away because of a mere dream:

> Then wherefore sully the entrusted gem
> Of high and noble life with thoughts so sick?
> Why pierce high-fronted honour to the quick
> For nothing but a dream?

His reply, if we think of it as coming as much from the developing Keats as from the love-sick Endymion, is of remarkable interest. 'Wherein lies happiness?' he asks, and he is in no doubt as to what ought to be the finally satisfying answer:

> In that which becks
> Our ready minds to fellowship divine
> A fellowship with essence till we shine,
> Full alchemiz'd, and free of space.

Leaving aside the derivation of those lines from Keats's philosophical reading, we can paraphrase them as meaning that happiness is a spiritual matter, finding its highest realization when the individual is so transfigured ('alchemiz'd') by 'fellowship divine' that he loses the sense of his physical being and becomes, in fact, 'free of space'.

Endymion then goes on to give an illustration of the manner in which this feeling of 'fellowship with essence' may be arrived at. The details of the process need not concern us. What does matter is the way in which it begins, and the condition to which it leads. This is the prescription for putting it in motion:

> Fold
> A rose leaf round thy finger's taperness,
> And soothe thy lips:

That, not to mention what follows, is rather irritatingly precious, and brings to mind Keats's own word 'mawkishness'. It is hard to resist the mental picture of an effeminate youth exquisitely, and absurdly going through the exercise. But that should not be allowed to distract us from what is really important here, and that is the fact that a process which is supposed to lead to spiritual transfiguration begins, not merely with the physical, since that is inevitable for human beings, but with deliberately calculated *sensation*. Laughable though they may be, the lines are vividly sensuous, almost to the point of the voluptuous. Their slight absurdity, indeed, comes partly from one's feeling that sensation is here being elevated into a ludicrously exquisite cult.

The end of the transfiguring process, on the other hand, is far removed from the physical:

> Feel we these things?—that moment have we stept
> Into a sort of oneness, and our state
> Is like a floating spirit's.

This is the state that has earlier been described as 'Full al- chemiz'd, and free of space'. But a new element has made its appearance. The end of the process brings us 'Into *a sort of oneness*'. What does Keats mean by this? The most obvious answer is that 'oneness' signifies the kind of 'fellowship divine' we have heard of already. That is to say, 'oneness' means 'oneness with essence'. Yet, as in other parts of this curious poem, the literally obvious meaning does not completely satisfy. Here it is by no means certain that 'oneness' signifies oneness *with* anything. Coming as it does immediately before the caesura, the whole phrase, 'a sort of oneness', has a finality and completeness in itself. It seems to refer not so much to oneness with something as to a sense of oneness *in the self*, a sense of integration, harmony, and balance.

To assert that this is what Keats primarily meant to say is no more possible than it is to be dogmatic about the word 'health' at the opening of the poem. Keats seems to be following a line of argument which makes one interpretation obvious, but which cannot exclude another. And the other interpretation, oddly enough, though it does not fit the argument so neatly, is by far the more compelling.

To say this is once again to point to the fundamental im- maturity of the poem. Keats is not sure exactly what he means. On the other hand, this very uncertainty makes the under-surface meaning particularly striking and important. For what Keats is essentially pursuing, in himself and in his work, is 'a sort of oneness'. We have already observed, in our examination of parts of *Endymion* and also of earlier poems, that much of Keats's early poetry reveals tensions springing from contradictory feelings and ways of looking at experience—tensions which have not as yet been brought under control. To bring them under control will mean recognizing that one set of feelings and appetites cannot merely be rejected in favour of another. 'Luxury' cannot simply be shoved aside to be instantly replaced by 'the agonies, the strife Of human hearts', for the dismissed appetites are not sent packing by such brusque action, but only pushed round the corner, where they lurk in readiness for the right moment to reinstate themselves. No, control means recognizing the nature of the warring feelings at the root of tension, and seeking in some way to come to terms with them. And it is this kind of control that will bring Keats to the 'sort of oneness' which he achieves in the great odes.

Returning to Endymion's speech, we can find in it some of the most important of the warring feelings. Like many writers before and after him, Keats is worried by the tension between the physical and the spiritual. One reason for this is doubtless that he was a young man highly susceptible to the promptings of the physical senses in all their forms. Another is that although he rejected institutional religion, he was convinced that there existed a kind of reality transcending the physical. In the passage that we have under consideration, Keats is trying to reconcile the physical and the spiritual by making physical sensation, here rather absurdly characterized, the beginning of a process which leads to 'a sort of oneness', in which 'our state Is like a floating spirit's'. We shall have occasion to recall this when we come to discuss the ode *To Autumn*.

Endymion, we must remember, is giving what ought to be the finally satisfying answer to the question 'Wherein lies happiness?'. But it is not finally satisfying for him. To achieve 'fellowship with essence' may be supremely desirable. He is, however, a human being, and for the human being

> there are
> Richer entanglements, enthralments far
> More self-destroying, leading, by degrees,
> To the chief intensity: the crown of these
> Is made of love and friendship, and sits high
> Upon the forehead of humanity.

> All its more ponderous and bulky worth
> Is friendship, whence there ever issues forth
> A steady splendour; but at the tip-top,
> There hangs by unseen film, an orbed drop
> Of light, and that is love:

Here we are conscious of tension between the spiritual 'oneness' and the alluring attractions held out by contact with other human beings—attractions which, in the case of sexual love, involve an ecstatic delight in the physical rather than a turning away from it. Keats is in no doubt as to the dangerous nature of such allurements. They are 'Richer *entanglements*', suggesting a snare; and 'enthralments' which are 'self-destroying', where the syntax allows us to interpret the words as meaning either that the enthralments destroy themselves by their very nature, or that they destroy the self of the individual who is enthralled. In the *Ode on a Grecian Urn* Keats will speak of 'human passion . . . That leaves a heart high-sorrowful and cloy'd', and will consider as an alternative to it the enduring beauty of a work of art. The words Endymion uses to characterize friendship, 'ponderous and bulky worth', likewise suggest a comparatively enduring value, even though friendship is here only half opposed to love, as it belongs to the same basic category.

Be that as it may, Endymion is not prepared to accept life without the joys of love. Indeed, the very words in which friendship is praised imply at the same time a criticism of it, for 'ponderous and bulky' suggest something heavily ungraceful, however estimable in its 'steady splendour'. Love is described as a radiance in which 'we blend, Mingle, and so become a part of it'. And whatever the perils to which men expose themselves by walking into love's entanglements, Endymion

> would rather be struck dumb,
> Than speak against this ardent listlessness:

'Ardent listlessness'; this time it is love which is implicitly criticized in the very words that voice Endymion's enthusiasm.

We need not go on to follow him through the justification of his feelings about love. What is far more important is to note that the feelings are ambivalent, and that they foreshadow Keats's different approaches to the subject of love in the *Ode to Psyche* and the *Ode on a Grecian Urn*.

It is in passages like the one which we have been discussing that the 'allegorical' significance, if we can call it that, lies, and not in the mechanics of the poem's plot. And it is certainly in such passages that the reader will find most of what is interesting in *Endymion*. One might go on to examine several others in the same way; but there is richer material ahead of us, and the scope of this book does not permit further detailed scrutiny of what is, after all, a relatively minor work in itself. Let us leave the poem by illustrating, from a passage in Book II, that taste for Spenserian 'decoration' so characteristic of one side of Keats, and so lavishly exploited in *The Eve of St Agnes*:

> Long he dwells
> On this delight; for, every minute's space,
> The streams with changed magic interlace:
> Sometimes like delicatest lattices,
> Cover'd with crystal vines; then weeping trees,
> Moving about as in a gentle wind,
> Which, in a wink, to watery gauze refin'd,
> Pour'd into shapes of curtain'd canopies,
> Spangled, and rich with liquid broideries,
> Of flowers, peacocks, swans, and naiads fair.

That, like other 'broideries' scattered throughout *Endymion*, may fairly be described as 'sensuous'. Its sensuousness, however, is a very different thing from that which gives life to the *Autumn* ode, in which Keats is not 'decorating', but rather catching the sensuous impact of autumn itself in the meaning and movement of his words.

Isabella (1818), *The Eve of St Agnes*, and *Lamia* (both belonging to 1819), are much smaller in scope than *Endymion*, and more directly concerned with story-telling. If these narrative poems have tended on the whole to receive a little less than justice in modern times, it is because they lack the kind of intricacy and density which makes the *Ode to a Nightingale* acceptable to the reader who enjoys Gerard Manley Hopkins and the seventeenth-century Metaphysical poets. Yet to slight them is a great mistake, for they belong to the main stream of Keats's development, and one of them, *The Eve of St Agnes*, is a success of a unique kind. The concern with vivid incident and dramatic 'atmosphere' in these poems reminds us that Keats had the ambition to become a dramatist. Despite his faith in his ability to achieve eventual greatness in the poetry of the theatre, his actual experiments in the genre do not encourage one to believe that his conviction was especially well-founded. What is wrong with his dramatic essays is that, like Wordsworth's, Shelley's, and Tennyson's assaults on the poetic stage, they contain patches of accomplished and effective verse, but are radically undramatic. To say this is to recall that the tradition of the English poetic drama had been virtually dead since the seventeenth century. No nineteenth-century poet was soaked in the very atmosphere of the theatre, as were Shakespeare and Ben Jonson, and their attempts at the poetic drama therefore result in poetry *applied to* the theatre, like an appendage, rather than poetry *of* the theatre. Merely to put verse into the mouths of characters on the stage was not enough to revive the tradition. Shelley's *The Mask of Anarchy* and Tennyson's *Ulysses* are more essentially 'dramatic' in their effect than *The Cenci* or *Becket*.

Keats's belief that he had it in him to write great plays springs from the tensions and dissatisfactions that we have been observing in his work. He wishes to leave behind him the purely personal, to involve himself in 'the agony, the strife Of human hearts', and where, he feels, can such things be more finely explored than in the drama? The narrative poems we now have under review are the product of the same urge. They show a determination to enter into the minds of others, to turn away from the selfish pleasures of exquisite sensation, to try to feel as others feel. Keats is not simply reforming his art: he is also striving to make himself into a better, because more complete, person. These poems thus play an important part in his efforts to achieve 'a sort of oneness'.

There is more to say about this. Achieving 'a sort of oneness' means coming to terms, as we have seen, with persistently nagging tensions. The narrative poems exhibit one side of this process.

In them Keats puts some of these tensions outside himself, as it were, taking them from the sphere of his own personal conflicts and embodying them in the predicaments of fictitious characters in a story. All three poems are about love; unhappy love in *Isabella* and *Lamia*, happy love (though this will need some qualification later on) in *The Eve of St Agnes*. Through them Keats examines his own feelings about love in particular and human experience in general. The poems are therefore, like so much in Keats, paradoxical. Springing from a desire to escape from the personal, they are at the same time a means of probing intensely personal feelings.

Isabella, 'A story from Boccaccio', is the story of the love of Isabella and Lorenzo, the resentment of the girl's brothers, who have destined her for a more brilliant match, their secret and brutal murder of Lorenzo, and the strange, unforeseen consequences, which lead to their flight from Florence and give the poem its sub-title, 'The Pot of Basil'. The poem is remarkably plain in its language, with none of the Spenserian tapestry-weaving to which we have grown accustomed in the youthful Keats. On the whole, the painful tale is simply and directly told. The poetry may not be of extraordinary distinction when scrutinized locally; but its directness comes as a relief after the overworked embroidery of *Endymion*:

> With every morn their love grew tenderer,
> With every eve deeper and tenderer still;
> He might not in house, field, or garden stir,
> But her full shape would all his seeing fill;
> And his continual voice was pleasanter
> To her, than noise of trees or hidden rill;
> Her lute-string gave an echo of his name,
> She spoilt her half-done broidery with the same.

There is no hint of coming pathos here. The tone of the poet is one of sympathy, yet it is also one of delicate amusement, perhaps most obviously so in the last line. The fact that it is Isabella's 'broidery' that gets spoilt is oddly appropriate, as though Keats were demonstrating how much more absorbing are the elemental human passions than the taste for decoration to which he has himself been so prone.

Keats is indeed careful to eschew pathos in the early part of the tale. The pair suffer torments before they confess their mutual love, but the tone of very slight amusement is sustained. And, just before the lovers' fortunes begin to turn, the poet explicitly denies any suggestion of making pathetic capital out of their situation:

> Were they unhappy then?—It cannot be—
> Too many tears for lovers have been shed,
> Too many sighs give we to them in fee,
> Too much of pity after they are dead,
> Too many doleful stories do we see,
> Whose matter in bright gold were best be read;

Keats seems deliberately to be weening himself away from 'mawkishness'.

In the next stanza, however, the coming tragedy is mentioned, though without portentousness . The reference to the fate of the lovers, in fact, is less interesting than what is said here about love in general:

> But, for the general award of love,
> The little sweet doth kill much bitterness;
> Though Dido silent is in under-grove,
> And Isabella's was a great distress,
> Though young Lorenzo in warm Indian clove
> Was not embalm'd, this truth is not the less—
> *Even bees, the little almsmen of spring-bowers,*
> *Know there is richest juice in poison-flowers.*

I put the last two lines in italics because they point forward to the stanza from the *Ode on Melancholy* which we glanced at in the first chapter:
> and aching Pleasure nigh,
> Turning to poison while the bee-mouth sips:

The *Ode on Melancholy* is a poem in which Keats is particularly successful in coming to terms with his predilection for 'luxury' in its most debilitating form. In it a sense of 'oneness' is achieved with what seems at first to be the most unpromising material for an undertaking whose end is harmony and equipoise. The lines from *Isabella* represent an important step in this direction. Not especially striking in themselves, they yet show a more conscious awareness of the likeness as well as the difference between pleasure and pain than anything in the earlier work, where the same general kind of feeling is mistily adumbrated in notions like that of dying a death of luxury.

This sharpening sense of the complexity of human feeling is one manifestation of Keats's revolt against 'mawkishness'. (*Isabella* was completed some two weeks after he wrote the Preface to *Endymion*.) Another is the calculated violence of the stanzas in which Isabella's brothers are denounced, a violence which reminds one of similar effects in Tennyson's *Maud*:

> Why were they proud? Because their marble founts
>   Gush'd with more pride than do a wretch's tears?—
> Why were they proud? Because fair orange-mounts
>   Were of more soft ascent than lazar-stairs?—
> Why were they proud? Because red-lin'd accounts
>   Were richer than the songs of Grecian years?—
> Why were they proud? again we ask aloud,
> Why in the name of glory were they proud?

In the more vitriolic passages of *Maud* one is conscious of a straining after vigorous effect which leads at the worst to melodrama and at the best to something less impressive than what was intended. Keats is a more forceful poetic personality than Tennyson (though, as we shall see, there are important points of contact between the two poets), and his bouts of violence are consequently rather more convincing; but he has the same tendency to collapse into bathos at awkward moments. The stanza we have quoted builds up an effective rhetorical case against the brothers until the last two lines are reached, whereupon the whole structure totters. After the question 'Why were they proud?' has been asked for the fourth time, the reader expects a grand climax of denunciation. All he gets, however, because it is apparently all that Keats can think of, is limp repetitiveness:

>   again we ask aloud,
>   Why in the name of glory were they proud?

But to lay too much emphasis on such shortcomings would be unfair, for the impulse behind them has led Keats far from the 'prettiness' of *Endymion*, even though the direction may in this case be a mistaken one.

The real weakness of *Isabella*, indeed, is to be found less in such lapses than in something which comes as a surprise in a poet aware of 'mawkishness' in his earlier work, and that is a vein of sentimentality. Lorenzo is dead, his spirit has appeared to Isabella, and she has retrieved his head and buried it in a pot of basil which she waters with her tears. The story is lurid enough in all conscience, yet Keats does not overdo the gruesomeness to the point of absurdity, as he might very easily have done. Unfortunately he is not content to let the story speak for itself now that the gruesome events have been narrated. After carefully avoiding pathos in the early stages of the poem, he feels that it is time to open the sluice:

> O Melancholy, linger here awhile!
>   O Music, Music, breathe despondingly!
> O Echo, Echo, from some sombre isle,
>   Unknown, Lethean, sigh to us—O sigh!
> Spirits in grief, lift up your heads, and smile;
>   Lift up your heads, sweet Spirits, heavily,
> And make a pale light in your cypress glooms,
> Tinting with silver wan your marble tombs.

And the pattern is repeated with variations three stanzas from the end of the poem. If we object to all this, it is not on account of indifference to Isabella's sorrow, but rather because, through heavily underlining it by somewhat wearisome repetitions designed to arouse a mood of anguish, such verbal gesticulation actually detracts from the pathos of the story.

Yet even this, on reflection, can be seen to play its part in Keats's development. For one thing, the attempt to arouse pity for Isabella, though unnecessary and unconvincing, is an aspect of his effort to enter into 'the agony, the strife Of human hearts'. He will be more successful later on. Furthermore, in addition to the link with the *Ode on Melancholy* which we noted early in the poem, there is here a direct foreshadowing of the ode's theme. In dwelling so heavily, almost lovingly, on the sorrow of Isabella, Keats is indulging in a kind of 'luxury'; indeed, it is his evident luxuriating in imagined woe that makes one call these utterances 'sentimental'. The *Ode on Melancholy* will take indulgence as its very subject.

The Eve of St Agnes, an infinitely finer poem than *Isabella*, has none of that work's defects. Indeed, although not on the level of the finest odes or *The Fall of Hyperion*, it deserves to be reckoned among Keats's most assured performances. 'Performance' strikes one as the right word for this poem, for it is a *tour de force* which, despite the generally high esteem in which the work has long been held, has not always been recognized for the remarkable thing it is.

The actual story narrated in *The Eve of St Agnes* is far more slender than the plot of *Isabella*. Fair Madeline retires to sleep on St Agnes' Eve, having been told by 'old dames' that on this night of the year

> Young virgins might have visions of delight,
> And soft adorings from their loves receive
> Upon the honey'd middle of the night,
> If ceremonies due they did aright;

To her comes young Porphyro; she wakes; and the lovers steal from the castle into the wind and sleet of a stormy morning. There is little more to the story than that. But nobody, one imagines, has attributed this poem's effectiveness primarily to its story. Much praise, however, has been bestowed upon the poem's building up of atmosphere, and the richness of its visual effects. If such praise, though completely justified, has not often gone to the root of the poem's distinction, it is because the exact nature of the 'atmosphere' and the function of the visual richness have not always been recognized.

I remarked earlier in this chapter that *The Eve of St Agnes* is a poem in which Keats's taste for Spenserian 'decoration' is lavishly exploited. It certainly contains some of his most gorgeous appeals to the visual imagination, like stanza XXIV:

> A casement high and triple-arch'd there was,
> All garlanded with carven imag'ries
> Of fruits, and flowers, and bunches of knot-grass,
> And diamonded with panes of quaint device,
> Innumerable of stains and splendid dyes,

> As are the tiger-moth's deep-damask'd wings;
> And in the midst, 'mong thousand heraldries,
> And twilight saints, and dim emblazonings,
> A shielded scutcheon blush'd with blood of queens and kings.

We note that Keats is once more using the Spenserian stanza; yet this poem is not simply a more mature imitation of Spenser. The gorgeousness is not there for its own sake, but has a particular function in the organization of the whole work, a function that is mainly a matter of contrast with effects that are not gorgeous at all. Thus to say that Spenserian decoration is here lavishly exploited should not be taken as meaning that this is the predominant impression left by the poem. The lavishness is there when Keats needs it. To the attentive reader, however, the impression left is of a complex blend, in which the gorgeousness is one element.

Contrast and its attendant device, parallel, both very deliberately worked out, are the foundation of this poem. It begins by stressing the intense cold of the night:

> St Agnes' Eve—Ah, bitter chill it was!
> The owl, for all his feathers, was a-cold;
> The hare limp'd trembling through the frozen grass,
> And silent was the flock in woolly fold:

The cold without is contrasted with the brilliantly illuminated interior, where revelry is about to commence:

> Soon, up aloft,
> The silver, snarling trumpets 'gan to chide:
> The level chambers, ready with their pride,
> Were glowing to receive a thousand guests:
> The carved angels, ever eager-eyed,
> Star'd, where upon their heads the cornice rests,
> With hair blown back, and wings put cross-wise on
>   their breasts.   (Stanza IV)

Later, in stanza IX, the cold without is contrasted with another kind of warmth within:

> Meantime, across the moors,
> Had come young Porphyro, with heart on fire
> For Madeline.

The glowing colours of stanza XXIV, which in themselves have the effect of suggesting warmth, are in fact thrown from the stained-glass of the casement by 'the wintry moon'. And in stanza XXXI Porphyro's sumptuous offerings to his lady, which are described in words whose brilliance carries associations of warmth, are explicitly contrasted with the chill:

> These delicates he heap'd with glowing hand
> On golden dishes and in baskets bright
> Of wreathed silver: sumptuous they stand
> In the retired quiet of the night,
> Filling the chilly room with perfume light.—

The 'carved angels' of stanza IV are, of course, part of the elaborate decoration of the castle's interior, and in that way link up with the 'carven imag'ries' of the casement in stanza XXIV. But there is more to be said about them than that, for these 'carved angels' are both linked with and contrasted with other references to angels; contrasted because, being merely part of a decorative scheme, they have no religious significance. In stanza XXV, on the other hand, when Porphyro sees Madeline kneeling at prayer, she is likened to an angel, with all the Christian associations of the word:

> Rose-bloom fell on her hands, together prest,
> And on her silver cross soft amethyst,
> And on her hair a glory, like a saint:
> She seem'd a splendid angel, newly drest,
> Save wings, for heaven:

And Porphyro bids her wake in these words:

> 'And now, my love, my seraph fair, awake!
> Thou art my heaven, and I thine eremite:' (Stanza XXXI)

The 'old beldame' who conducts him to Madeline's chamber is both amused and appalled at her lady's belief in the superstition surrounding St Agnes' Eve:

> 'St Agnes' Eve!
> God's help! my lady fair the conjuror plays
> This very night: good angels her deceive!' (Stanza XIV)

Urging Porphyro to leave, she has this to say:

> 'A cruel man and impious thou art:
> Sweet lady, let her pray, and sleep and dream
> Alone with her good angels, far apart
> From wicked men like thee.'   (Stanza XVI)

Moreover, the old woman's name is *Angela.*

Now, all these references to angels are connected with one most important element in the poem, and that is its mingling of the Christian with the secular and even with the pagan. The very superstition that sends Madeline early away from the revellers to seek her chamber is a piece of thoroughly pagan folk-belief, and, as such, most oddly associated with the Christian Saint Agnes. To give another example, stanza V, which begins with the influx of the 'argent revelry', goes on like this:

> These let us wish away,
> And turn, sole-thoughted, to one Lady there,
> Whose heart had brooded, all that wintry day,
> On love,

The use of the capital 'L' for Madeline is a daring stroke, which, although not explicitly conferring upon her a sanctified status, tends to connect her in our minds with the saint for whose favours she will pray that night. In stanza VII we hear of her 'maiden eyes divine'; and stanza IX tells how Porphyro longs to

> gaze and worship all unseen;
> Perchance speak, kneel, touch, kiss—in sooth such
> things have been.

We notice how the idea of worship soon gives way to that of physical contact. It is no accident that this is so, for Porphyro, though he later calls Madeline his 'seraph fair', stands very much for the human and unsanctified.

To return to the opening of the poem, there is mention of quite a different Lady in the lines from stanza I which describe the devotions of the Beadsman:

> Numb were the Beadsman's fingers while he told
> His rosary, and while his frosted breath,
> Like pious incense from a censer old,
> Seem'd taking flight for heaven without a death,
> Past the sweet Virgin's picture, while his prayer he saith.

50

The Beadsman, a 'patient, holy man', represents orthodox
Christianity at its most austere. If St Agnes' Eve is an occasion
for hope in the case of Madeline, it is another matter for him:

> His was harsh penance on St Agnes' Eve:
> Another way he went, and soon among
> Rough ashes sat he for his soul's reprieve,
> And all night kept awake, for sinners' sake to grieve.
>
> (Stanza III)

The contrast could hardly be more extreme. Not only, of course,
is it the contrast between austerity and hoped-for ecstasy: it
is also the contrast between youth and age. The flight of the
lovers at the end of the poem is for them the beginning
of a new life. The Beadsman, on the other hand, is linked
with death from the start:

> already had his deathbell rung;
> The joys of all his life were said and sung: (Stanza III)

He is not the only representative of age in the poem to die as the
lovers fly into the future. There is also Angela, the 'old beldame':

> Angela the old
> Died palsy-twitch'd, with meagre face deform;
> The Beadsman, after thousand aves told,
> For aye unsought-for slept among his ashes cold.
>
> (Stanza XLII)

Though hardly an austere figure like the Beadsman (we recall her
chuckles at the thought of what Madeline is doing, shocked though
she may be), Angela's judgment of superstition is in line with the
beliefs of a good Christian. At the same time, we may suspect her
of having a vein of superstition, and of being precisely the kind of
old woman who has given Madeline the story of St Agnes' Eve.
Whatever the truth of the case, there is plainly no room for either
Angela or the Beadsman at the end of the poem. The former dies
repulsively 'palsy-twitch'd', while there is a sardonic tone in the
reference to the latter's 'thousand aves'. The poet's comment
seems to be that the only world which matters is the world into
which the lovers have flown. Angela and the Beadsman belong to
a dead past.

If those two aged figures represent religious orthodoxy both at its most extreme and its most ordinary levels, Madeline's position is midway between Christianity and paganism. Although she courts 'St Agnes' saintly care', and prays with all the appearance of devout Christianity, her very belief in the superstition is non-Christian. And this is the place to point out that Madeline and Porphyro's love for her are associated with what has for centuries been a symbol of beauty both heavenly and earthly, both spiritual and carnal—the rose:

> Rose-bloom fell on her hands, together prest,   (Stanza XXV)

>> Blinded alike from sunshine and from rain,
> As though a rose should shut, and be a bud again.
>>>> (Stanza XXVII)

> Sudden a thought came like a full-blown rose,
> Flushing his brow, and in his pained heart
> Made purple riot: (Stanza XVI)

> Into her dream he melted, as the rose
> Blendeth its odour with the violet,—
> Solution sweet: (Stanza XXXVI)

For all Madeline's devotion, it is the earthly, physical aspect of the rose that will win the day. When she flies with Porphyro from the castle, we feel that she is leaving the spiritual aspect behind with the dead bodies of Angela and the Beadsman.

We have now to consider the special function of her lover. It is Porphyro, hated by Madeline's family, who carries her off into a new life. Put like that, his role sounds very much that of the conventional romantic lover rescuing his lady fair from her wicked kindred. Yet this view of him is not supported by attentive reading of the poem. For one thing, though he may be execrated by Madeline's kindred, there is no concrete reason to assume that she suffers at their hands. Furthermore, her elopement with Porphyro is an equivocal business.

Consideration of this takes us to the heart of the poem. Madeline is in love with Porphyro, certainly; it is obviously of him that she is thinking when she goes through the ritual of St Agnes' Eve, and she flies with him at the end without the slightest hint of protest. In a way, however, Angela is right to call him a 'cruel man', for although he brings his lady the love that she craves, he wakes her to face with him a world whose reality may prove—what? Bitter? Disillusioning? Or simply mingled in its pleasure and pain? Keats does not give us an answer, but he does tell us that 'These lovers fled away *into the storm*'. Their new life, whatever it may bring them, begins with no glamorous sunrise. The poet is careful to emphasize this. In stanza XXXVI, with Madeline awake but not yet knowing whether her lover truly stands before her or not, the storm begins:

> meantime the frost-wind blows
> Like Love's alarum pattering the sharp sleet
> Against the window-panes; *St Agnes' moon hath set.*

I put the last words in italics, because the moonlight has up to this point been a pervasive presence in the poem from the first appearance of Porphyro in stanza IX, 'Beside the portal doors, Buttress'd from moonlight'. While giving an atmosphere of richly romantic enchantment, it has at the same time been linked with a kind of unreality. We are not meant to suppose that the casement glowingly described in stanza XXIV is in any literal sense 'unreal'. It is as real as the two lovers, not just part of a dream. But both the moonlight and the gorgeousness evoked in the most famous stanzas of the poem *go with something that Madeline has to leave behind if she is to follow her lover*. This is true in spite of Porphyro's own contribution to this romantic richness, the dainties that he heaps in his lady's chamber:

> And still she slept an azure-lidded sleep,
> In blanched linen, smooth, and lavender'd,
> While he from forth the closet brought a heap
> Of candied apple, quince, and plum, and gourd;
> With jellies soother than the creamy curd,
> And lucent syrops, tinct with cinnamon;
> Manna and dates, in argosy transferr'd
> From Fez; and spiced dainties, every one,
> From silken Samarcand to cedar'd Lebanon.   (Stanza XXX)

For all those exotic delights are put there only to be left. There is nothing glamorous about the 'flaw-blown sleet' and 'iced gusts' into which the lovers must fly. As they steal to the castle's door, the tapestries and carpets (those embodiments of the Spenserian side of Keats) are agitated by the wind:

> The arras, rich with horseman, hawk, and hound,
> Flutter'd in the besieging wind's uproar;
> And the long carpets rose along the gusty floor. (Stanza XL)

It is as though Keats were saying that the decorative fancy, to which he has himself given such rein in this very poem, is at the mercy of a reality much stronger than tapestries and carpets.

This is the reason why the 'gorgeousness' of *The Eve of St Agnes* must be seen in its proper perspective. Magnificent though it may be, it is something from which 'These lovers fled away', just as the poet himself, though not turning his back upon it, has put it to superbly functional use in a poem whose overall effect is far from merely decorative.

What is the significance of this strange work? Is it an attack upon institutional Christianity, a celebration of earthly joys at the expense of religious orthodoxy? Is it a kind of hymn in praise of the pagan? It is certainly not the latter, for if one sees the poem as a dismissal of Christianity one must also see it as a dismissal of paganism. Madeline is certainly granted her 'soft adorings', but this has nothing to do with her performance of superstitious rites. Porphyro merely takes advantage of what Angela tells him about Madeline's intentions. *He* is no prey to superstition, as we learn from stanza XV, moved though he is by 'his lady's purpose':

> and he scarce could brook
> Tears, at the thought of *those enchantments cold*,
> And Madeline asleep *in lap of legends old*.

(My italics.) Nor is it really possible to view the poem as an attack on Christianity pure and simple. Both Christianity in its pure form, and in its adulterated, 'paganized' form, are part of the world on which the lovers turn their backs, yet it would be a mistake to suppose that Keats is merely *dismissing* beliefs that he does not share. For although Angela and the Beadsman may die, and Madeline may be roused to a new world of reality, the storm into which the lovers fly is pregnant with ominous possibilities. It is not a flight into a glamorous never-never land, but a step into the coldly real. Thus, despite his sardonic thrust about the Beadsman's 'thousand aves', Keats does not offer the lovers' flight as a triumphant escape from a world of superstition, both institutional and pagan, into an illuminated landscape in which everything is for the best. What Keats is doing is to explore in a most subtle manner the tension between the spiritual and the physical, and the ambiguous nature of love.

Lamia has not the close organization of *The Eve of St Agnes*, and consequently demands less comment. It is, however, related to that poem in theme. Telling the story of the serpent assuming the shape of a beautiful woman who wins the love of Lycius, a Corinthian youth, only to be exposed for what she is by the youth's mentor, Apollonius, in the midst of the bridal feast, *Lamia* is concerned with the fragility of love and the impermanence of human happiness in general. One might say that the subject of the poem is 'Beauty that must die', a beauty that is symbolized partly by Lamia herself, partly by the happiness of the pair before Lamia makes the fatal mistake of bowing to her lover's wish to display his mistress to the world, and partly by the miraculously wrought entertainment that she magically prepares for her unwanted guests. As in *The Eve of St Agnes* the gorgeous visual effects, such as we find in this passage from Part II, are entirely functional:

> A haunting music, sole perhaps and lone
> Supportress of the faery-roof, made moan
> Throughout, as fearful the whole charm might fade.
> Fresh carved cedar, mimicking a glade
> Of palm and plantain, met from cither side,
> High in the midst, in honour of the bride:
> Two palms and then two plantains, and so on,
> From either side their stems branch'd one to one
> All down the aisled place; and beneath all
> There ran a stream of lamps straight on from wall to wall.

The point of all this is that it is nothing but a false appearance, none the less beautiful for being false, but doomed to destruction from the moment the eye of Apollonius is cast upon Lamia. Yet it is essential to realize that the poet does not invite us to condemn Lamia, serpent though she is. Rather are we made to pity her, and all those for whom joy must turn to poison. If there is any condemnation to be meted out, it is for Apollonius and the 'cold philosophy' he stands for.

4

THE ODES I

The Eve of St Agnes, *Lamia*, and the odes, all belong to the great creative year of 1819. It is hardly surprising, then, that there are links between all seven of these poems, though some of these may not be immediately obvious. To trace a single, consistent, and chronological line of development from poem to poem would be extremely convenient; it is not, however, really practicable. The poems come so close together, the writing of one being inevitably affected by work upon another, that it is not truly useful or possible for the commentator who wishes to increase understanding and enjoyment of them to arrange them in a strict chronological order. *Lamia*, for instance, must strictly be regarded as later than the odes; yet to say for this reason that it represents an advance upon them, or a development out of them into something quite new in Keats, would be thoroughly misleading. All one can usefully do is to examine the poems in the order which seems most likely to assist the reader in grasping them, even though that order may not exactly coincide with the dates on which individual poems are known to have been completed. Rather than trying to see the poems as a single stem, so to speak, let us treat them as a number of separate shoots all springing from the same root and nourished by the same soil.

The *Ode on Melancholy*, now that we have considered the narrative poems, makes a good point of departure for further discussion. We have seen hints of its theme in earlier work, its technique has been forshadowed in the paradoxes of *Endymion*, and we have observed that the subject of *Lamia* is suggested by words from this ode itself—'Beauty that must die'; not to mention the lines which follow:

> And Joy, whose hand is ever at his lips
> Bidding adieu; and aching Pleasure nigh,
> Turning to poison while the bee-mouth sips:

The lines take us back, moreover, to other work that we have already examined, for we are reminded by 'Joy' and 'Pleasure' of the 'luxuries' the poet conjures up in *I stood tip-toe*, and the 'joys' to which he says he must bid farewell in *Sleep and Poetry*. *The Eve of St Agnes*, superficially a poem of entirely happy love, has a connection with this aspect of the ode. There is no knowing what the lovers may have to face in the world into which they flee, a world whose possibly sinister potential is suggested by the storm which takes the place of the moonlight. May they not, like Lycius and Lamia, find that joy deserts them?

The idea of impermanence; the notion of human joy as a desperately fragile, transient thing; the conviction that happiness, at its very height, must inevitably turn into something else— these provide the data, as it were, from which Keats begins in the *Ode on Melancholy*. Not that the poem literally opens with the expression of such sentiments. On the contrary, they are explicit only in the last stanza; but the whole ode has been built upon the assumption that they are justified. The poem is concerned with coming to terms with what are in themselves depressing feelings by trying to find a means of making them bearable.

The means proposed is an odd and, at first glance, a somewhat repellent one. Keats apparently recommends nothing less than whole-hearted indulgence in one's sorrows, a point of view which must strike readers who have grown up to believe that one should control one's emotions rather than give way to them as weak-spirited and even positively contemptible. Certainly a superficial description of the poem to one who has never read it is likely to make him suspect that it is an unpardonably sentimental piece of work. After all, abandoned indulgence in sorrow, so that one actually revels in the idea of being unhappy, is a mark of that worst kind of sentimentality which is closely akin to insincerity. It indicates that the sorrow to which the writer abandons himself is very far from being genuine, being merely the result of pressing various emotional buttons to produce the 'right' sort of reaction both in himself and in his reader. But the *Ode on Melancholy* is no more sentimental than are certain other poems, such as Emily Brontë's *Remembrance* and D. H. Lawrence's *Piano*, which give an initial impression of being so. If both those poems triumphantly escape the charge of sentimentality it is because the writer in each case registers sturdy resistance to the seductive temptation to give way. Lawrence does abandon himself at the end of his poem, but only while simultaneously recognizing that he ought to be doing nothing of the kind. *Piano* is not sentimental in either of the two most common ways. It does not unintelligently and weakly wallow in what in itself may be perfectly respectable sentiment; and, on the other hand, the very strength of the resistance put up tells us that the emotion fought against is genuine. We feel that the poem succeeds because of the writer's character and intelligence.

The *Ode on Melancholy* equally represents a triumph of character and intelligence, though they manifest themselves in rather different ways. To begin with, although the poem registers resistance, it is not resistance to melancholy itself but to the temptations which melancholy brings in its train:

> No, no! go not to Lethe, neither twist
> > Wolf's-bane, tight-rooted, for its poisonous wine;
> Nor suffer thy pale forehead to be kiss'd
> > By nightshade, ruby grape of Proserpine;
> Make not your rosary of yew-berries,
> > Nor let the beetle, nor the death-moth be
> > > Your mournful Psyche, nor the downy owl
> A partner in your sorrow's mysteries;

In other words, do not try to escape from your sorrows by resorting to narcotics, oblivion, and suicide, surrounding yourself with all the classic appurtenances of gloom and death. (The allusion to Psyche will strike the reader as more meaningful when we have discussed the ode to that goddess. For the time being it is enough to understand the reference as meaning that we should not abandon ourselves to death and its associations with the rapture of Cupid giving himself to Psyche.) So far this advice is on the whole eminently in line with what one has been told about moral fortitude, keeping one's sorrows in check, and so on. But the concluding lines of the first stanza give reasons for the advice that are extremely remote from the tradition of the stiff upper-lip:

> For shade to shade will come too drowsily,
> And drown the wakeful anguish of the soul.

To seek easy escapes from sorrow is a mistake, not because it is unmanly, or immoral, or impious—but because it prevents one from experiencing 'the wakeful anguish of the soul' to the full! Melancholy, then, is not to be resisted. It is to be vividly *felt*.

This sounds unpromising in a poem which has earlier been described as representing a triumph of character and intelligence. One word in the last line, however, suggests a reason why the stanza as a whole, despite its odd sentiments, does not seem morbid or debilitating in general effect: the word 'wakeful'. On the purely literal level, of course, the word points to the state Keats regards as desirable for the proper impact of sorrow, and contrasts with the idea of going to Lethe. At the same time, 'wakeful' is aptly descriptive of a state of mind and an attitude towards language apparent in the stanza. We have found Keats paradoxical on previous occasions; paradox is well to the fore once again. The conclusion of the stanza, taken by itself, would seem to be advocating a singularly perverse view of things. Going in for one's sorrows to the full—could anything be more eccentric or unhealthy?

Yet the final lines do not account for the effect of the stanza as a whole. Far from having an air of spinelessness, it is remarkably alive and muscular. The reiterated negatives, paradoxically enough, spring from a strongly positive belief in the value of life and the futility of attempted flight from what is distressing:

> No, no! go not to Lethe, neither twist
> Wolf's-bane, tight-rooted, for its poisonous wine;

If the aliveness is evident in the emphatic manner in which easy escapes are ruled out at the very beginning of the poem, it can also be seen in the masterful handling of language. Here we have something utterly distant from the exquisitely decorative verbal weaving of Spenser. Keats's feeling for the relationship between language and sensation makes us rather think of Shakespeare. In articulating the words 'neither twist Wolf's-bane, tight-rooted', the reader experiences a tongue-twisting sensation as he finds his way round the consonants which parallels and enacts part of the meaning. And the close conglomeration of consonants in the mouth suggests the tightness of the plant's roots. It is this kind of effect which makes one use the word 'muscular' to describe the impression made by the stanza, and lends a peculiar aptness to the adjective 'wakeful'. Keats may end by prescribing a seemingly perverse view of existence. We feel, none the less, that he is thoroughly 'awake' to life and the necessity to live.

The sense of upsurging life is abundant in the second stanza, which, on the evidence of the first line, is the most unlikely place in which to find it:

> But when the melancholy fit shall fall
> Sudden from heaven like a weeping cloud,
> That fosters the droop-headed flowers all,
> And hides the green hill in an April shroud;

Keats is about to tell us what to do when melancholy descends. From what he has said at the end of the previous stanza, one might well expect the 'wakeful anguish of the soul' to issue either in something brooding, at one extreme, or passionately sorrowful at the other. What actually comes is entirely different. The word 'weeping', to be sure, accords with one's expectations; but its use in the context conjures up associations that are quite unlooked-for. It is a *cloud* that is referred to as weeping, not a person, and the effect of the sudden shower of rain is to refresh and give renewed life to 'the droop-headed flowers', which have been hanging their heads for lack of water. The reader who has never experienced an April shower in England should know that such a downpour often comes with remarkable suddenness. Instead of coming on gradually, with increasing intensity, the rain can descend quite heavily all of a sudden, leaving off soon afterwards with the same abruptness. Observe that the onset of the shower is here enacted by the poet's use of his verse-structure. The stress on 'Sudden' given by its position at the beginning of line two, reinforced by the pause at the end of the previous line, gives the very effect of the rain's unexpected descent.

The fourth line carries very mixed associations. 'Shroud' suggests death and funerals; yet 'green hill' evokes a feeling of brightness and freshness, going with the traditional idea of April, in a temperate climate, as standing for youth and renewal of life.

Keats is therefore speaking of melancholy in terms of a simile which makes it seem, on the whole, to be life-bringing rather than depressing. Does he really mean this? Are we asked to believe that a 'melancholy fit' should be regarded as a pleasurable experience bringing with it a sense of new vitality? In a perfectly obvious way, he means nothing of the kind. He is not literally telling us that melancholy leads to vitality. He is not making any statement to that effect. What he does is to employ imagery that holds suggestions of freshness and renewal. The impression which results from this is a complex one, the conventional associations of 'weeping' and 'shroud' being balanced by 'fosters' and 'green hill'. It is Keats's way of conveying to us his sense of the inextricable mingling of the pleasurable and the painful in human existence. He does not mean that vitality and melancholy are one and the same, or anything so plainly stupid as that. He is simply implying that, human life being the complex thing it is, melancholy and vitality, like many other apparent opposites, are more closely related than one might ever have imagined. And in doing this, he is preparing the ground for his confrontation of life's paradoxes in the final stanza.

It is in the remainder of the second stanza, however, that we reach the centre of the ode, and are able to recognize what is truly its theme:

> Then glut thy sorrow on a morning rose,
>> Or on the rainbow of the salt sand-wave,
>> Or on the wealth of globed peonies;
> Or if thy mistress some rich anger shows,
>> Emprison her soft hand, and let her rave,
>> And feed deep, deep upon her peerless eyes.

The first four lines of the stanza having accustomed the reader to Keats's technique of setting disparate associations side by side, he is not surprised to find 'sorrow' in company with the brightness of 'morning rose' (where thoughts of the fresh morning light and the colour of the rose are combined), 'rainbow' (which gives us all the colours of the spectrum), and 'globed peonies' (cup-shaped flowers of a beautiful crimson hue). What he may also have noticed is the presence of certain tell-tale words: 'glut', 'wealth', 'rich', 'And feed deep, deep'. I call them tell-tale words because they put us immediately in mind of Keats's abiding predilection for 'luxury'. And we observe that the poet, far from turning his back upon 'luxury' in these lines, is recommending positive indulgence in it, with sorrow as the prime ingredient. 'Then *glut* thy sorrow', 'And *feed deep, deep*'—the heavy stresses imparted by the rhythm, and the additional emphasis given to key-words by the dominant -*ee*- sound, leave us in no doubt that Keats is prescribing a surfeit. 'Here, then', he seems to be saying, 'is the best way of bearing one's sorrows. Do not run away from them. Since sorrow has to be borne, why not luxuriate in it instead?'

But is Keats really saying quite that? Certainly a sense of the absolute inevitability of sorrow is part of his meaning, as the final stanza will make clear. Certainly, too, he is unblushingly proposing indulgence, not as a means of escaping from pain, but as a way of putting up with it. We must make sure, however, that we know just what it is that Keats recommends us to indulge in. The last three lines of the stanza, which might seem the easiest to interpret from this point of view, are ambiguous:

> Or if thy mistress some rich anger shows,
> Emprison her soft hand, and let her rave,
> And feed deep, deep upon her peerless eyes.

If the poem ended there, the lines could readily be taken as referring to a physically real 'mistress', the woman with whom one is in love, and whose 'anger' is among the contributory causes of one's sorrow. But what immediately follows in the last stanza is this:

> She dwells with Beauty—Beauty that must die;

Who is 'She'? It is hard not to identify her with the 'mistress' of the preceding lines, yet impossible not to see her five lines later as a personification of melancholy itself:

> Ay, in the very temple of Delight
> Veil'd Melancholy has her sovran shrine,

The 'mistress' may thus be regarded as either a 'real' woman, a personification of melancholy, or both. At all events, the poet plainly urges the reader to luxuriate in and draw positive sustenance from the experience, whether we take it as being the 'rich anger' of his lady, or the descent of the 'melancholy fit' at its most intense.

So far we have seen nothing in this to qualify the assertion that Keats is frankly advocating indulgence in sorrow as the best means of facing it. If we go back to the previous three lines, however, we notice a significant difference in the things mentioned. The mistress very easily becomes the lady Melancholy of stanza III; but no such transformation awaits the rose, the rainbow, or the peonies. We cannot say that the poet is advocating indulgence in these things, for they can hardly be said to offer anything to be indulged *in*, beyond their beauty. Indeed, the word 'glut' notwithstanding, Keats is not precisely advocating indulgence at all in these lines.

What then does he mean by the injunction to 'glut' one's sorrow on those colourful things which seem to consort so oddly with it? How can a person vent his sorrow on inanimate objects like flowers, let alone a mere apparition such as a rainbow? In strict truth, Keats is not suggesting that he can. Explaining the matter concisely, if a trifle obscurely, one might say that the state of superabundant emotion brought about by the 'melancholy fit' can lead to and expend itself in a heightened awareness of the beauty of natural sights in the world around one. In other words, the emotional 'charge', generated by melancholy, is directed to the contemplation of such things as the rose, the rainbow, and the peonies. The feeling of melancholy may begin in a vague, undefined way; by expending itself upon something real and visible outside the person who suffers from it, the feeling is transformed, and, since it can no longer be called sorrow, is thereby conquered.

So we see that Keats is offering two different ways of coming to terms with one's sorrows. One may simply indulge in them up to the hilt; or they may be transformed through being directed at the contemplation of natural beauty, in which case, despite

Keats's vocabulary, they cannot be described as leading to indulgence. In each case the emotion seeks an object, whether it be the 'globed peonies' or the 'peerless eyes' of the mistress; and in each case, either by transferring itself to contemplation of the object or by drawing a melancholy sustenance from it, the emotion is modified. One may truthfully speak of the 'peerless eyes' of the mistress as constituting an object, despite the fact that the next line turns her into a personification, for in stanza two she is quite human and real. Indeed, it is the stress upon the object, upon what is in the most ordinary sense real, that gives this stanza much of its strength. We find here that vivid response to the physical world which often seemed thwarted in the early work by the tendency to lapse into 'pleasant smotherings', and which will achieve its apotheosis in the ode *To Autumn*.

It must be admitted, however, that the raving mistress, her soft hand imprisoned by her lover's, has somewhat the air of a figure in romantic melodrama. I have known certain readers to be so irritated by this that they have been unable to take the poem seriously. Now such a response is mistaken, for Keats has not been guilty here of an error of taste or judgment. He knows exactly what he is doing, and how far he can go. He is proposing two ways of coming to terms with one's sorrows, distinct from one another, but built into the unity of the stanza by a vocabulary which makes them appear superficially the same. The first of the ways directs the contemplation to the beauty of the physical world. If this be called 'luxury', there is nothing unhealthy or enervating about it. Keats may speak of 'the *wealth* of globed peonies', but he also gives us 'the *salt* sand-wave'. There is no room for the tang and bitterness of 'salt', or anything so down-to-earth, in the kind of experience that leads to swooning, or to 'pleasant smotherings'. In the second of the two ways Keats does unblushingly offer indulgence as a remedy, and here we do feel the presence of something repellent in this kind of 'luxury'. But Keats knows this. Going as far as he dare go in this picture of the melancholy lover drawing a perverse satisfaction from the eyes of his raving mistress, he stops just on the right side of absurdity, and swiftly transforms the lady into what will turn out to be a personification.

Keats is now ready to face the sad truth about human existence as he sees it. For general comment on the meaning of the stanza we refer the reader back to Chapter 1. The fact that pleasure and pain, joy and sorrow, are inextricably mixed, conveyed to us implicitly in stanza II, is here explicitly stated. A few points are worth mentioning in addition to those made in the first chapter. We have commented on the way Keats uses verse-structure in the image of

> Joy, whose hand is ever at his lips
> Bidding adieu;

There is more to be said about the pause after 'lips'. If we think about the effect of the words 'Bidding adieu' in their position just after the pause, it is difficult not to experience a mental picture of a person turning momentarily to us as he walks away, making the gesture of farewell. Consider also the man

> whose strenuous tongue
> Can burst Joy's grape against his palate fine;

Once again Keats uses language to enact meaning, for there is an effect here similar to that which we found at the very beginning of the poem. The oral movements made by the reader in articulating the words clearly aloud, so that the consonants are properly detached from each other, suggest the effort made by the tongue to press the grape against the roof of the mouth so hard that it bursts. In the lines which follow, and conclude the whole poem, there is an especially subtle instance of Keats's manner of bringing home to us the connection between joy and melancholy:

> His soul shall taste the sadness of her might,
> And be among her cloudy trophies hung.

When 'Joy's grape' bursts, the mouth must be filled with a gush of juice. But what the person whose strenuous tongue has done this actually tastes is not joy at all. He savours instead 'the sadness of her might'; that is to say, the sad power of melancholy. Capable of enjoying the most intense happiness, his soul is fated to be numbered among the 'trophies' that are hung up in her temple to betoken her victories.

Can we sum up the meaning of this ode? Certainly not in a neat paraphrase, for, apart from some of the last stanza, the poem works in ways which resist such an approach and can only be dealt with, as we have seen from our examination of stanza II, by inevitably heavy-handed commentary. The poem must be viewed as an organic structure, in which parallels and contrasts within the whole are as much part of the meaning as the statement that 'She dwells with Beauty'. Thus Keats's use of a word like 'glut', which suggests indulgence, when he is hardly speaking about indulgence at all but rather about an alternative to it, is an important contribution to the meaning, for the poet does not wish us to settle for the simple view that he is merely recommending luxurious abandonment to sorrow. In the context of the second stanza, the word plays its part in defining the manner whereby the impulse to indulge may be directed away from personal sorrow to the heightened contemplation of beautiful things in the world outside. Keats is indeed centrally concerned in this ode with the directions that an impulse which he knows to be strong within himself can take, and he is not afraid candidly to include luxurious abandonment among them—though the somewhat melodramatic words in which he writes of it, so different from what we find both before and after, imply his own criticism of such a course. 'To feed deep, deep . . . Well, that is *one* way,' we might imagine Keats saying, 'but there are other ways, and they are probably more valuable.' It is this subtle treatment of an impulse profoundly typical of him, together with the superb vitality of language which triumphantly counters all suggestion of the morbid, that give this poem its remarkable distinction.

If indulgence is the central theme of the *Ode on Melancholy*, it is not the only one. Nor is this poem alone among the odes in treating of it. The temptation to indulge in morbid desires figures in the *Ode to a Nightingale*, and resistance to this may be regarded as the climax of the poem:

> Now more than ever seems it rich to die,
>   To cease upon the midnight with no pain,
>   While thou art pouring forth thy soul abroad
>   In such an ecstasy!
>   Still wouldst thou sing, and I have ears in vain—
>   To thy high requiem become a sod.

VII
Thou wast not born for death, immortal Bird!
No hungry generations tread thee down;
The voice I hear this passing night was heard
In ancient days by emperor and clown:
Perhaps the self-same song that found a path
Through the sad heart of Ruth, when, sick for home,
She stood in tears amid the alien corn;

In rejecting the wish to die, Keats repudiates any connection between the nightingale and the very idea of death itself. He does not, of course, mean that the bird is literally 'immortal', but he takes the nightingale's song, the song of innumerable nightingales reaching back over the centuries to 'ancient days', as a symbol of permanence. Generations pass, like 'this passing night', yet the song of the nightingale endures from age to age. We have seen, on the other hand, that it is impermanence, the idea that beauty and joy are fragile and transient, that provides the data, as we have called it, for the *Melancholy* ode. The final stanza of that poem, by linking melancholy explicitly with this idea, makes us realize that the conviction of impermanence is the real source of 'the melancholy fit'. The *Melancholy* ode accepts impermanence as inevitable, and even implies that one can make a virtue out of this. After all, to 'glut thy sorrow on a morning rose', etc., suggests that pain can turn into pleasure, just as pleasure can turn to poison.

But the *Ode to a Nightingale* rebels against such a view. For the Keats of this poem, the passing of youth, happiness, and beauty cannot be accepted without a struggle. The thought of it fills him rather with horror and depression, keenly registered in stanza III, which contrasts the nightingale 'among the leaves' with the realm of human existence

Where palsy shakes a few, sad, last gray hairs,
Where youth grows pale, and spectre-thin, and dies;
Where but to think is to be full of sorrow
And leaden-eyed despairs;
Where Beauty cannot keep her lustrous eyes,
Or new Love pine at them beyond to-morrow.

In this ode, the 'melancholy fit' cannot be cured either by a redirection of emotional energy or by downright indulgence, both of which imply an acceptance of sorrow, even though it be a rueful one. Nothing can lift the pall of depression except faith in the possibility that something may endure, that there may be at least some way of believing that beauty does not always die. And it is towards such a belief that Keats strives in the *Ode to a Nightingale*.

No poem of this author is more full of his characteristic tensions, nor in any poem are they turned to more superb account. Here Keats recognizes them absolutely for what they are, and builds great poetry out of them. The tendency to lapse away into a kind of swoon, the impulse to give up the battle by seeking oblivion, dominates the opening:

> My heart aches, and a drowsy numbness pains
> My sense, as though of hemlock I had drunk,
> Or emptied some dull opiate to the drains
> One minute past, and Lethe-wards had sunk:

The key-words, 'aches', 'drowsy numbness', 'pains', 'dull opiate', 'Lethe-wards had sunk', produce a cumulative effect of drugged languor, aided by the movement of the verse. In the first line the caesura after 'aches' is so pronounced a break that the rest of the sentence seems to be picked up with difficulty. This is so because, quite apart from the comma and the fact that a complete statement has been made in those three words before the pause, the ensuing word 'and' has to be carefully detached from the preceding word if the articulation is not to sound slovenly. The halting movement which results suggests the poet's languid state. Consider also, following this, the handling of the run-on line. The pause which we must make after 'pains', since this is a line-ending, despite the onward progress of the sentence, breaks the meaning in such a way that 'My sense' comes out a little later than we would expect, giving us the impression that in his benumbed state the poet is too drowsily inactive mentally for the words to emerge without fumbling delay. And the run of the meaning is picked up after those words with the same laboured heaviness that we found in the corresponding place in line one.

Similar effects produced by the use of the caesura and the run-on line are to be seen in lines 3 and 4.

Now, it is true that Keats does not speak of himself as literally encouraging the feelings conveyed in the opening lines. The very fact that they come to him, however, not to mention the evidence of later stanzas, reveals a morbid, 'deathly' emotional tendency. For the feelings seem particularly perverse in the light of what gives rise to them. Does the poet feel like this because he is envious of the nightingale's happiness? Apparently not:

> 'Tis not through envy of thy happy lot,
> But being too happy in thy happiness,—
> That thou, light-winged Dryad of the trees,
> In some melodious plot
> Of beechen green, and shadows numberless,
> Singest of summer in full-throated ease.

It is an excess of happiness, brought about by entering into what he imagines to be the happiness of the bird, that has occasioned the poet's mood. His mood notwithstanding, the words 'happy' and 'happiness' cannot help causing a change of feeling in the reader. There comes a sense of refreshment after the narcotic drooping of the first four lines, a feeling of renewed life, announced by 'light-winged'. This contrasts vividly with the heaviness of what has gone before, and the new brightness is carried on in 'beechen green' (where the colour of the beech trees carries the same associations of freshness as 'green hill' in the *Ode on Melancholy*), 'shadows numberless' (where 'shadows', although in some contexts a sombre word, suggests the luxuriant foliage by which the shadows are cast), 'summer' (with all its associations, in a temperate climate, of colour and warmth), and 'full-throated ease'. 'Ease' is almost the last word that one would expect to find at the end of this stanza, considering its languid, halting start. One feels that the very mood of the poet has changed, as he thinks of the nightingale and the 'melodious plot' in which it sings. Has he been wrong, after all, in believing that an excess of happiness has brought on his depression?

The brightness certainly appears to continue in the second stanza:

> O, for a draught of vintage! that hath been
> Cool'd a long age in the deep-delved earth,
> Tasting of Flora and the country green,
> Dance, and Provençal song, and sunburnt mirth!
> O for a beaker full of the warm South,
> Full of the true, the blushful Hippocrene,
> With beaded bubbles winking at the brim,
> And purple-stained mouth;

The nightingale and its song seem to have given way to other thoughts, taking their origin from the word 'summer'—thoughts of wine, the colourful lands in which its grapes are grown, and the gaiety which it brings. A general atmosphere of warmth predominates; 'sunburnt mirth' combines the idea of the sun's warmth with the warmth of high spirits in the merrymaker. There is one touch of delicious contrast in the second line, where the thought of coolness is reinforced by 'deep-delved earth', suggesting shady depths far removed from the baking sun of 'the warm South'. (Notice that the alliteration hints at the strokes of the spade digging into the earth.) Then suddenly the whole atmosphere changes, and we see the reasons behind the poet's craving for 'a draught of vintage':

> That I might drink and leave the world unseen,
> And with thee fade away into the forest dim:

III

> Fade far away, dissolve, and quite forget
> What thou among the leaves hast never known,
> The weariness, the fever, and the fret
> Here, where men sit and hear each other groan;

And there follow the lines, quoted earlier, about the inevitable decay of youth and beauty, and the attendant flight of happiness.

The reader finds that *he*, rather than the poet, has been mistaken, for the brightness of the lines that have gone before turns out not to have betokened a real change of mood, but has merely been a product of the excessive happiness that Keats links with his depression. The happy and pleasant thoughts connected with wine were simply a kind of 'waking dream', and the real reasons for his craving have never been far away. His longing for wine does not mean a thirst for warmth and gaiety: it expresses a desire for oblivion, a yearning to 'fade away into the forest dim'. Wine is sought as an 'opiate', or even as a poison like hemlock. We are back to the mood of the first stanza, or at any rate the mood in which it began. In this frame of mind, Keats would certainly not resist the temptation to 'twist Wolf's-bane, tight-rooted, for its *poisonous wine*'. He would not resist it, that is, were there not a spring of vitality in him which even the most gloomy thoughts cannot permanently subdue. It is this vitality which makes the poem, for in it we have that upsurging feeling for life that pulls against the longing to 'fade away' either 'to Lethe' or 'the forest dim', for it does not matter what one calls it, the impulse is the same. It means oblivion, one way or the other.

We realize now why Keats has not been wrong in attributing his depression to 'being too happy in thine happiness'. The nightingale is imagined to be happy *because it is not human*, because it has never known 'The weariness, the fever, and the fret' of human existence. And the poet knows too well that the happiness he feels in mentally following the bird into its world 'among the leaves' cannot last, for he is a human being after all, and what is human must pass away. His depression is thus implicit in the happiness itself.

But in the fourth stanza the poet tries vigorously to pull himself together. Gloomy thoughts about the human lot are brusquely dismissed, together with the possibility of wine ('Bacchus and his pards') as an alternative to them. Keats will now seek refuge in poetic fancy:

> Away! away! for I will fly to thee,
>   Not charioted by Bacchus and his pards,
> But on the viewless wings of Poesy,
>   Though the dull brain perplexes and retards:

Notice the enactment of meaning in the fourth line, where the two successive stressed syllables, 'dull brain', and the slightly awkward articulation of 'perplexes and retards', do indeed 'retard' the movement. The 'dull brain' notwithstanding, poetic fancy wings the poet swiftly to the nightingale in its perch up among the tree-tops, where the moon and stars can be seen:

> Already with thee! tender is the night,
>   And haply the Queen-Moon is on her throne,
>   Cluster'd around by all her starry Fays;

Doubtless poetic fancy is here working very prettily, but there is something decidedly affected and precious about the reference to the 'Queen-Moon', and the idea of the stars as fairies. Keats is being self-consciously 'poetical' in the bad sense, as though he had gone back to the 'pretty' manner of *Endymion*. It is not accidental that he has used the rather affected word 'Poesy' here. The lines are exceedingly charming, and when we have said that, we have made a point against them. This kind of 'charm' is not what we have come to expect from the mature Keats.

In fact the affectation is quite deliberate, for 'the viewless wings of Poesy' turn out to be just as ineffectual as the chariot of Bacchus. Poetic fancy does not last long. No sooner are the three pretty lines over than Keats is on the ground again, back to the reality about him. He has come from the tree-tops down to earth, where the 'Queen-Moon' and 'her starry Fays' are not to be seen:

> But here there is no light,
> Save what from heaven is with the breezes blown
>   Through verdurous glooms and winding mossy ways.

The implied comment is that 'Poesy', as represented by the previous fanciful lines, is too flimsy a thing to afford much in the way of sustenance. The light which reaches the poet down here on the earth is not the imagined steady radiance of the 'Queen-Moon' but only the small glints of moonlight fitfully seen as the breeze parts the branches. Notice how the tangle of the verdure and the winding of the 'mossy ways' are brought home by the effect of the words in the third line of the quotation.

Stanza v shows that delighted response to the sensuous beauty of the physical world that we have found in varied contexts from the earliest work of Keats onwards. We must emphasize, however, that the poet is not in this stanza describing what he actually *sees* around him. He tells us explicitly that there is not enough light for him to distinguish the flowers growing on the ground and the blossoms on the trees and hedges. He can only guess what they are from their scents. But this is not the same thing as the previous poetic 'fancy', for the workings of his imagination are here rooted in a thoroughly solid notion of what the invisible blooms are like. The language has its peculiarities, as we shall observe, yet it is quite without the affectation of 'Poesy':

> I cannot see what flowers are at my feet,
>   Nor what soft incense hangs upon the boughs,
> But, in embalmed darkness, guess each sweet
>   Wherewith the seasonable month endows
> The grass, the thicket, and the fruit-tree wild;
>   White hawthorn, and the pastoral eglantine;
>   Fast fading violets cover'd up in leaves;
>   And mid-May's eldest child,
>   The coming musk-rose, full of dewy wine,
>   The murmurous haunt of flies on summer eves.

The pretty fancies of 'Poesy' would find little or no place for anything so extremely down-to-earth as 'The grass, the thicket, and the fruit-tree wild'. Even the last line of the stanza, the most 'poetic' in the sense of using verbal resources not habitually exploited in prose, deals with something far removed from delicate whimsies about 'starry Fays'. The flies are real flies; and if the line is 'poetic', it is because the last few words, through their sound when spoken aloud, give us an idea of the thin, 'murmurous' noise made by those insects.

The language of the stanza, as I have remarked, has its peculiarities. These can be located in the contrast between such homely words as 'the seasonable month', and '*soft incense*', '*embalmed* darkness', 'dewy *wine*'. We know, of course, that Keats is literally referring to the scent of the flowers and the nectar of the musk-rose. But the words are such as to conjure up thoughts of 'luxury'; and 'wine', we have come to feel, is a danger-signal in this poet.

We are right, for stanza VI gives us Keats at his most morbid. All the swoonings and luxuries of his earlier work seem to have been leading to this:

Darkling I listen; and for many a time
I have been half in love with easeful Death,
Call'd him soft names in many a mused rhyme,
To take into the air my quiet breath;

And then come the lines in which he feels that it would be '*rich* to die, To *cease* upon the midnight *with no pain*'. It will be noticed that the emphasis is upon what is 'soft' and 'easeful'. Death is courted, not as abrupt extinction or lingering demise, but as painless dissolution. The poet once more wishes to 'Fade far away' and 'dissolve'. We see now that the '*soft* incense' of stanza v, though it literally refers to something quite different, contains a hint of this mood, and that the 'dewy *wine*' of the musk-rose has brought the idea of oblivion back to the surface of the poet's consciousness. Keats could hardly be more open in a declaration of what we have for some time perceived to be 'deathly' tendencies. He now sees the morbid impulse clearly for what it is.

Yet an important point must be made. Keats is only 'half in love with easeful Death'. I spoke not long ago about this poet's unquenchable vitality, and, paradoxically enough, it is nowhere more apparent than in this stanza. For it is this upsurging feeling for life that makes him sweep aside the luxurious thought of its being 'rich to die'. There would be no 'richness' about it at all. The bird would go on singing, whilst he, having become merely a lifeless 'sod', would no more be able to enjoy its song.

And so Keats moves on to his affirmation of a belief in permanence, in an enduring principle of life, a belief symbolized by the song of the nightingale, heard by countless generations over the centuries. The generations pass, but they cannot silence the nightingale's voice. Keats's imagination ranges back across the years to the time when emperors had their court-jesters, who could hear the nightingale's song just as their regal masters did; to the far-distant days of the Old Testament, represented by the story of Ruth; and at last, in the astonishing conclusion of the stanza, to something yet more remote:

The same that oft-times hath
Charm'd magic casements, opening on the foam
Of perilous seas, in faery lands forlorn.

Simply to sit back and gasp admiringly at the mysterious beauty of these lines, as so many readers must have done, is not enough. Mysterious and beautiful they certainly are, yet do they not mean something? To say, in so many words, just what they do mean would be extraordinarily difficult. Keats has gone as daringly far as he can go in the direction of pure suggestion, where statement hardly seems to count. What are these 'magic casements', these 'perilous seas' and 'faery lands'? Why, for that matter, are the seas 'perilous', and the lands 'forlorn'? We cannot say. Explaining the lines as meaning that the bird's song has often inspired tellers of fairy stories, though it conveys a small part of the truth, does not account for anything like half of their effect. And attempts to trace the origins of the lines in the poet's reading of other men's work, while such an approach is interesting and enlightening in many ways, cannot finally help us. The only manner in which we can properly analyse the lines is by considering the suggestive properties of the words themselves. As happens so frequently in Keats, the effect depends upon telling contrast. Here it is contrast between the enchantment and mystery suggested by 'Charm'd', 'magic', and 'faery', the emotionally disturbing associations of 'perilous' and 'forlorn', the visual impact of 'foam' (a frothy white patch in the midst of all the vagueness), and the very homely word 'casements'—casements which seem literally to open at the caesura in the penultimate line, for the observer to gaze forth upon the waves.

Is there nothing more to the lines, then, but vague suggestion? If not, can they be called good poetry? There *is* more to the lines, if we look at them in their context. Keats has been roving back down the ages. He has spoken of the 'ancient days' of recorded history, and the far-off times of the Bible. Now, with great daring, he hints at something profoundly buried, yet at the same time profoundly present in all of us—that world of the subconscious from which have issued so many aspects of the legends, superstitions, and customs of a race. The 'perilous seas' put us in mind of the sea on which the adulterous wife sets sail in *The Demon Lover*, or, to recall another ballad, 'the roaring of the sea' heard by the hero of *Thomas Rhymer*. The question of whether the lines are good poetry or not has perhaps now been answered. By themselves their suggestive power would be considerable, but it would be hard, if one met them divorced from their context, to make any pronouncement about their ultimate value. Mere potency of suggestion cannot make good poetry, and much fine modern work which might appear to depend entirely on suggestion will be found on examination to use context to give suggestive power the direction in which its impact can properly be felt, as Keats has used context here.

Having gone so far into the depths, where the 'casements' of his own consciousness have briefly opened upon something long buried, it is not surprising that the poet wakes up to his surroundings with something of a start:

> Forlorn! the very word is like a bell
> To toll me back from thee to my sole self!

Out of eighteen words in those two lines, only two have more than one syllable. The succession of monosyllables produces an effect of flat, 'prosaic' reality. Keats mentally bids the nightingale farewell, and with it the 'fancy' which has led him so far away from his 'sole self':

> Adieu! the fancy cannot cheat so well
> As she is fam'd to do, deceiving elf.

The bird's song being now 'buried deep In the next valley-glades', the poet asks himself

> Was it a vision, or a waking dream?
> Fled is that music:—Do I wake or sleep?

The lines are ambiguous in their reference, as are those concerning that '*deceiving* elf' the 'fancy', who 'cannot *cheat* so well As she is fam'd to do'. What is the experience of whose nature the poet is uncertain? In what way has fancy tried to cheat him? Does Keats mean the whole experience so far recounted by the poem, the entire series of feelings and counter-feelings? Has fancy tried to cheat him into believing that something which has not happened has taken place? Or is the poet referring only to the thoughts of stanza VII, where he sets up the nightingale as a symbol of permanence, of immortality? Is he dismissing those thoughts as merely idle whimsies?

There is no definite answer to those queries, for Keats has made his words deliberately ambiguous. The reason is that he is striving towards a satisfying conception of permanence. He has not really found it yet, though the song of the nightingale will do for the time being as an indication of the kind of thing he is looking for and trying to say. He is thus consciously tentative, and by leaving us in doubt as to whether or not he means that the fancy has been trying to cheat him in making him attach all that symbolic importance to a mere bird, he is offering that conception of permanence for our consideration, whilst acknowledging that we may well dismiss it.

5

THE ODES II

If the *Ode to a Nightingale* is tentative in its offering of a symbol for permanence, *Ode on a Grecian Urn* proposes something far more obviously enduring in a quite ordinary sense: a work of art. At the opening of *Endymion* Keats has told us that 'A thing of beauty is a joy for ever', and in this ode the thing of beauty is a Grecian urn of great antiquity, beautiful not only in its shape but also because of the scenes which the decorations on its surface exquisitely portray. Keats does not mean that the urn must literally last for ever, any more than he expects us to believe that one single nightingale has been singing ever since the time of the Old Testament, for the urn is in theory just as liable to destruction as any other object of man's making. But the fact that it has already endured for so long, and the likelihood that its antique beauty will entitle it to a care for its preservation which the majority of objects in this world do not receive, make it a peculiarly satisfying symbol of permanence.

The central significance of the ode is given us in the last stanza, where the poet, having addressed the urn as 'Cold Pastoral', goes on to say

> When old age shall this generation waste,
>   Thou shalt remain, in midst of other woe
> Than ours, a friend to man, to whom thou say'st,
> 'Beauty is truth, truth beauty,'—that is all
>   Ye know on earth, and all ye need to know.

We shall return to the famous words about beauty and truth in due course. What concerns us now is Keats's idea of the urn remaining 'in midst of other woe Than ours'. By this he means that although one generation of suffering human beings will be replaced by another generation, and so on over the years, the urn will continue to exist as it is, an unchanging thing of beauty in the midst of the changing woes of rising and passing generations.

The words 'Cold Pastoral' make a convenient starting-point for discussion of the poem. The urn is 'cold' in the very obvious sense that it is an inanimate object, without the warm blood of human life, and made of a substance which is normally cold. Its 'coldness', in this sense, is thus indissolubly linked with its power to endure, as opposed to the living and dying of 'warm' humanity. But there is more to be said about the 'coldness' of the urn, for it points to an aspect of its beauty implied at the very beginning of the poem:

> Thou still unravish'd bride of quietness,
> Thou foster-child of silence and slow time,

The words 'still unravish'd bride' strike an immediate note of surprise. This 'marriage' between the urn and 'quietness' is likened metaphorically to a human marriage that has never been consummated. The 'bride' retains her virginal purity. Not only is 'she' a partner in no physical union: it is implied that she is the 'child' of an equally non-sensual relationship— not the issue of 'silence and slow time', but their 'foster-child'.

These metaphors have the effect of stressing the calm, non-human purity and detachment of the urn. They prepare us for subsequent statements and suggestions of the urn's remoteness from what the poet regards as impure, unrewarding, and distressing in the human lot. The articulation of the words, especially in line 2, imposes a slow movement appropriate to the atmosphere of calm surrounding the precious object.

If the urn is more pure than humanity, it is also a better and sweeter story-teller than the human poet:

> Sylvan historian, who canst thus express
> A flowery tale more sweetly than our rhyme:

What this 'flowery tale' *means*, in a normal sense, is something that Keats cannot say. Do the scenes on the urn refer to men, or gods, or both? Where are the scenes supposed to be taking place? The scenes appear to depict people in particular situations, but what exactly *are* those situations?

> What leaf-fring'd legend haunts about thy shape
> Of deities or mortals, or of both,
>> In Tempe or the dales of Arcady?
> What men or gods are these? What maidens loath?
> What mad pursuit? What struggle to escape?
>> What pipes and timbrels? What wild ecstasy?

And the questions cannot be answered, for the 'Cold Pastoral' has nothing to utter but the teasing words about truth and beauty in the last stanza.

The second stanza tells us why the urn is regarded as a story-teller superior to the poet. No lines of Keats are more boldly paradoxical than these. The 'pipes and timbrels' have brought the idea of music into his mind, yet it remains no more than an idea, for these 'melodies' do not impinge upon the physical hearing:

> Heard melodies are sweet, but those unheard
>> Are sweeter; therefore, ye soft pipes, play on;
> Not to the sensual ear, but, more endear'd,
>> Pipe to the spirit ditties of no tone:

Because it appeals to the 'spirit' rather than to the gross 'sensual ear' of ordinary hearing, this music is thought of as being superior to that which may be heard in the normal way. We realize, therefore, that the fact that Keats cannot ascertain the precise meaning of the scenes depicted on the urn is to him a positive virtue in this work of art. It tells a story 'more sweetly than our rhyme' because, although the scenes may hint at specific situations, they are without all the gross human circumstances, the paraphernalia of 'what happened before and what came later', that must be handled by the human story-teller. The urn merely *suggests* situations.

The poet gives his attention to two scenes, or two parts of the same scene, which thus suggest situations easily imaginable as taking place in the real world. In the first we see a youthful musician, in the second a lover pursuing his maiden:

> Fair youth, beneath the trees, thou canst not leave
>> Thy song, nor ever can those trees be bare;
>> Bold Lover, never, never canst thou kiss,
> Though winning near the goal—yet, do not grieve;
>> She cannot fade, though thou hast not thy bliss,
>> For ever wilt thou love, and she be fair!

The poet is bringing home to us another quality in the work of art, which he considers to be a supreme virtue, and which is part of its value as a symbol of permanence. Whereas in 'real life' the youth would at last stop singing and the trees would lose their leaves in late autumn and winter, the scene represented pictorially on the urn cannot change. And although the lover can never capture his maiden, for they are both fixed parts of a motionless pattern, he should take comfort from the fact that his love for her likewise cannot change, nor will her beauty fade. All this is very different from the human world of the *Ode to a Nightingale*,

> Where Beauty cannot keep her lustrous eyes,
> Or new Love pine at them beyond to-morrow.

Keats handles movement to underline meaning in two striking places. Consider the words

> thou canst not leave
> Thy song,

The break in the sense occasioned by the pause after 'leave' might superficially suggest interruption of the song, and thus contradict the meaning. Reflection on the context, however, shows that a completely appropriate effect emerges. By breaking the flow of the sense in what may seem a rather arbitrary manner, Keats impedes the movement of the words, thus emphasizing the idea of the scene as fixed and immobile. There is a similar effect produced by the clogging repetition of 'never' in the next line, which likewise retards the flow and suggests the unchanging stance of the lover, caught for ever in a pursuit that can lead to no goal.

Stanza III dwells upon the thought of these changeless scenes. In *them*, at least, beauty does not die, pleasure does not turn to poison, joy is not perpetually bidding adieu:

> More happy love! more happy, happy love!
> For ever warm and still to be enjoy'd,
> For ever panting, and for ever young;

The repetition of 'happy' does not serve merely to fill out the line. Keats is drawing a distinction between ordinary human notions of 'happy love', and what he at the moment regards as the far more genuine happiness of the 'Bold Lover' portrayed by the urn. His love is 'happy' precisely because it is 'still to be enjoy'd', and will never attain consummation. By repeating 'happy', the poet stresses the unchanging continuity of this state. Human love in the real world, on the other hand, though it may be 'enjoy'd' in a physical sense, brings with it an aftermath of sorrow and satiety:

> All breathing human passion far above,
>   That leaves a heart high-sorrowful and cloy'd,
>   A burning forehead, and a parching tongue.

Notice the contrast between the feverishness of that last line and the general air of coolness and stillness surrounding the urn. We shall have more to say about the implications of the contrast when we come to review the overall significance of the ode.

In the fourth stanza, meanwhile, the urn is slowly turned around, so that other scenes are offered to our mental vision:

> Who are these coming to the sacrifice?
>   To what green altar, O mysterious priest,
>   Lead'st thou that heifer lowing at the skies,
>   And all her silken flanks with garlands drest?

The dominant word is 'mysterious', which not only refers to the priest and the rite he is going to perform, but describes the poet's feelings about everything that he mentions in this stanza. As in stanza I, he asks a series of questions which cannot be answered, the bafflement being an ingredient in the peculiar beauty of the urn. Why, for instance, have the populace deserted the 'little town' shown in one of the scenes? Once again Keats reminds us of the urn's changelessness:

> And, little town, thy streets for evermore
>   Will silent be; and not a soul to tell
>   Why thou art desolate, can e'er return.

Yet there is a definite difference between the feeling conveyed here and that communicated in the previous two stanzas. Whereas Keats has expressed nothing but profound envy for the changeless state of the 'Fair youth' and the 'Bold Lover', he seems at the end of stanza IV to introduce an unexpectedly mournful note. The strongly emphasized word 'desolate' cannot help carrying with it a feeling of sadness and chill. Why, then, is the poet not consistent? If he is glad that the lover, for example, can never win his maiden, why should he seem sorry that the little town can never again be peopled? Keats does not, to be sure, actually say that he feels sad about it, but the associations of 'desolate' are too strong to be ignored.

The last stanza gives us our answer. It does this by implication, just as the sense of sadness comes to the reader by implication. Stanza IV has ended by dwelling on a scene empty of human figures. This makes an ideal transition to the opening lines of the last stanza, which stress the non-human quality of the urn again and again:

> O Attic shape! Fair attitude! with brede
> > Of marble men and maidens overwrought,
> With forest branches and the trodden weed;
> > Thou, silent form, dost tease us out of thought
> As doth eternity: Cold Pastoral!

'*Shape*', '*attitude*', '*silent form*', '*Cold* Pastoral', whose surface is decorated with '*marble* men and maidens': one is almost tempted to say that the word for the urn, despite its beauty, is '*in*human' rather than '*non*-human', so icily chaste does it appear in those words. Yet one is not allowed to fall into that temptation, for Keats goes on explicitly to call the urn 'a friend to man'. How are we to reconcile these two differing ways of looking at the object, one which sees it as a friend to man, and another which implies that the urn is coldly remote from man?

Keats does not ask us to reconcile two views of the urn, by trying to pretend that they are not in conflict with each other. What he invites the reader to do is rather to weigh one view against the other, to balance the two sets of feelings towards the urn, so that finally they may be seen as complementary, though remaining distinct. There is loss as well as gain in the virginal purity of the beautiful object. For all that he says about the unrewarding nature of 'breathing human passion', Keats does not really wish to turn his back upon what is human, however unsatisfactory it may be. Perhaps the reader has already noticed something curious about the description of 'happy, happy love' in stanza III. The lover and his maiden are of marble, like all the other figures on the urn; yet their love is described as 'For ever _panting_', and 'For ever _warm_'. The poet is speaking of them as though they were alive, and could experience 'breathing human passion'. Yet at the same time he envies their changeless state of fixity in the marble pattern. He wants to 'have it both ways'— to combine the permanence of the work of art with the warmth of human life, provided that only the pleasant things in life are included. When the scene is empty of human figures at the end of stanza IV, he experiences a feeling of chill, and is as 'desolate' as the streets of the little town. The work of art may be exquisitely beautiful and satisfying as life can rarely if ever be; but life, in spite of its woes, has a warmth that insidiously creeps into the poet's contemplation of the marble figures. It is almost as though he were breathing life into them.

Yet the urn, while still being a 'Cold Pastoral', is 'a friend to man'. And here we have to consider those apparently oracular words "'Beauty is truth, truth beauty'". In point of fact they are not oracular at all; nor should they for one moment be attributed, as they commonly have been, to Keats himself. It cannot be too strongly emphasized _that they are imagined as being uttered by the urn_. Once this is grasped, all misgivings as to the value of the words as wisdom should disappear, for they are by no means offered as a supremely wise pronouncement. The urn, we have been told, _teases us_ 'out of thought As doth _eternity_'. By likening the urn to eternity, Keats both reinforces its value as a symbol of permanence, and tells us that it has the same capacity to divert us from rational thinking as bewilderment on the idea of eternity. The word 'tease' implies that the urn tantalizes the beholder. Precisely. It tantalizes him by suggesting an ideal state of things in which one might combine the permanence of art with what is purely pleasant in human life. But the beholder knows—as Keats knows—that this is no more than a suggestion. Once rational thought steps in, the formula 'Beauty is truth, truth beauty' ceases to work. 'Truth' to what? Not, assuredly, to the facts of life as actually lived; only to life as one may imagine it as conjured-up by the daydream of 'having it both ways'. Keats cannot be convicted of saying that living *should* be a perpetual daydream. He presents the ideal of permanent happiness as nothing more than a beautiful impossibility, which the urn as 'friend to man' may help us to see sometimes as a possibility. 'A friend to man' it is, at the same time coldly remote from man. The unchanging work of art has its own limitations, just as the changing world of transient human life has its virtues.

Keats does not come down heavily on the side of either Art or Life. The feelings of attraction and repulsion, felt in respect of both, meet and mingle in the poem to form an essential part of its total meaning. The tensions explored between them are dealt with in Keats's effort to achieve within himself 'a sort of one-ness'. Certainly he has achieved here a poem of superbly organized effect, which magnificently balances the claims of both the work of art and breathing human life. A work in which the controlling intelligence is well to the fore, it asks for intelligent reading, which it has not invariably received. Hence the absurd notion that it sets up a claim for an Absolute Beauty as a kind of religion, and that it advocates the doctrine of Art for Art's sake, when the truth of the matter is that Keats means 'Art for *Life*'s sake'.

Two important points will introduce the remaining odes to be discussed. The first concerns the question of 'breathing human passion'. When all is said and done, it cannot be denied that the *Ode on a Grecian Urn*, for all its balancing of art and life, does speak in notably disparaging terms of sexual love. The implied comment is that if only love could stop perpetually at the stage of mere desire, all would be well. This takes us back to the tension between the physical and the spiritual evident in our discussion of *Endymion*, and now explicitly recognized in the contrast between 'the sensual ear' and 'the spirit'. Though it brings Keats in the direction of 'a sort of oneness', this ode does not quite reach it. At the same time as admitting the claims of warm-blooded life, it seems to voice the feeling that sexual love is something of a disaster. The *Ode to Psyche* presents an altogether different view.

The second point relates to the idea of permanence. While Keats has found in the Grecian urn a more satisfying symbol for permanence than the song of the nightingale—though the *Ode to a Nightingale* is not for that reason an inferior poem—it is plainly not entirely satisfactory. In a way, the critical reservations implied about the claims of art tend to weaken its power as a symbol, for it is only too possible to prefer the warm impermanence of human life to the cold permanence of the urn. In the ode *To Autumn* Keats does not seek that kind of symbol. The ode is both the crown of his work, and a serene expression of belief in the inevitable rightness of the whole life-process, impermanence included.

Writing in April 1819, about the *Ode to Psyche*, Keats said that it was to that date the first poem in which he had taken 'even moderate pains'. While allowing for exaggeration, one does see that this ode has been put together in a highly deliberate manner. Two long outer stanzas enclose two that are both shorter and of a more 'formal' character, and there are consciously worked-out parallels and contrasts between the second and third stanzas and the first and fourth. The idea behind the ode is the Greek myth of Eros and Psyche, signifying the union of Love and the Soul. Psyche did not emerge as a goddess until well on in the history of ancient religion, hence Keats speaks of his poem as a tardy offering to one born 'too late for antique vows'.

The myth of Eros and Psyche naturally appealed to Keats as a symbol of one of the very things he was looking for—a resolution of the tension between sexual love and spiritual values. The ode triumphantly achieves such a resolution, but one must be careful about one's use of the words 'spiritual values' or 'the soul' in talking about this poem. Though not a fundamentally irreligious man, Keats adhered to no religious orthodoxy. It would therefore be absurd to attempt to identify his idea of the soul with that of any known religious pattern, Christian or pre-Christian. Attentive reading of the *Ode to Psyche* shows that one main theme of the poem is the nature of poetic composition itself. It is the only one of the odes in which Keats writes of himself as a practising artist. In quite a literal sense, the poem concerns his intention to create something, a temple dedicated to Psyche, for she became a goddess too late to have a temple dedicated to her by antiquity. But this temple is no ordinary building. It will be, as the last stanza tells us, a work of the devoted imagination:

> Yes, I will be thy priest, and build a fane
>> In some untrodden region of my mind,
> Where branched thoughts, new grown with pleasant pain,
>> Instead of pines shall murmur in the wind:

The whole of the last stanza, indeed, together with most of the third, can be read as an 'extended metaphor' referring to the creation of a poem. And the poem Keats creates is the very ode itself.

The poem begins by directly addressing Psyche, the third and fourth lines suggesting an intimacy of utterance that persists to the end:

> O Goddess! hear these tuneless numbers, wrung
>> By sweet enforcement and remembrance dear,
> And pardon that thy secrets should be sung
>> Even into thine own soft-conchèd ear:

Keats's verses are 'tuneless' literally because he does not sing them. He does not carry the 'lyre' referred to in stanza III. At the same time, the word 'tuneless' implies, if not actual harshness, a certain lack of grace or elegance. This impression is reinforced by 'wrung', which suggests that the 'numbers' have emerged with some unwillingness, or at any rate with a degree of difficulty. The suspension of the meaning after 'wrung', if we make the correct pause at the line-ending, adds to this feeling that the 'numbers' have not come out with glib smoothness, and the idea of unwillingness and hardship is carried on by 'enforcement', with the further notion of compulsion. Yet it is a '*sweet* enforcement', associated with 'remembrance *dear*', the remembrance clearly being that of the vision which Keats recounts in the rest of the stanza. The effect of these mingled suggestions is to imply that the writing of the poem has been, to use a cliché phrase, 'a labour of love'. The 'love' is evident in 'sweet' and 'dear', not to mention the warmth with which the poet speaks of Psyche from first to last. The 'labour', indicated by 'wrung' and 'enforcement', is simply the effort involved in giving adequate poetic expression to a new experience. If the numbers emerge with some unwillingness, the reluctance is in *them*, so to speak, rather than in the poet, who has to 'wring' them into some sort of shape corresponding with his vision.

The idea of literary effort reappears in the lines already quoted from the last stanza, where Keats describes the 'branched thoughts' which take the place of pine-trees around Psyche's imaginary temple as being 'new grown *with pleasant pain*'. Artistic creation is far from being a painless process, however 'pleasant', 'sweet', or 'dear' the feelings which have given rise to it. The poet tells Psyche, moreover, that her temple will be built 'In some *untrodden region of my mind*', which links up with 'new grown' to indicate that the poetic effort implied here is the outcome of an experience entirely new and fresh.

The experience itself is given in the first stanza. Keats tells how he was wandering 'in a forest thoughtlessly',

> And, on the sudden, fainting with surprise
> Saw two fair creatures, couched side by side
> In deepest grass, beneath the whisp'ring roof
> Of leaves and trembled blossoms, where there ran
> A brooklet, scarce espied:

The woodland setting of the vision is a parallel to the imagined surroundings of Psyche's temple in the last stanza, surroundings which refer metaphorically to the workings of the poet's mind in giving shape to his experience. The 'branched thoughts' become metaphorically the trees which cover the slopes of the wild mountains, and recall the forest of stanza I:

> Far, far around shall those dark-cluster'd trees
> Fledge the wild-ridged mountains steep by steep;
> And there by zephyrs, streams, and birds, and bees,
> The moss-lain Dryads shall be lull'd to sleep;

To fledge means literally 'to furnish with feathers' (in the case of birds), and therefore, more generally, 'to clothe'. The 'branched thoughts' which are the new growth of poetic effort will thus cover a landscape that has previously been wild and barren. By metaphorically 'planting' these mountainous steeps, and introducing 'nurture' into the landscape, Keats suggests that imposition of fertile order upon previously intractable poetic material which is of the essence of artistic achievement. Notice the enactment of meaning in the adjacent consonants of 'dark-cluster'd', and the impression of jagged skyline given by the rough articulation inevitable in 'wild-ridged mountains'.

To return to stanza I, Keats is not sure that he really has *seen* the vision:

> Surely I dreamt to-day, or did I see
> The winged Psyche with awaken'd eyes?

'Awaken'd' is an interesting word here, for there is more to it than the simple distinction between sleeping and waking. The vision of the 'two fair creatures' has come to him with the force of a startling revelation, which is why the poet describes himself as 'fainting with surprise' when coming upon them. But the ending of the stanza makes it plain that the surprise is not simply a matter of unexpectedly seeing two beings he had not thought of meeting at that moment. For he immediately knows the identity of one. It is only after questioning himself, however, that he recognizes the other:

> The winged boy I knew;
> But who wast thou, O happy happy dove?
> His Psyche true!

The sight of Eros has not in itself occasioned him particular astonishment. What has really amazed him, it is clear, is the presence of Psyche in the embrace of 'the winged boy'. Keats does not try to disguise the frankly physical manifestation of their love, immortal though they be:

> 'Mid hush'd, cool-rooted flowers, fragrant-eyed,
>   Blue, silver-white, and budded Tyrian,
> They lay calm-breathing on the bedded grass;
>   Their arms embraced, and their pinions too;
>   Their lips touch'd not, but had not bade adieu,
> As if disjoined by soft-handed slumber,
> And ready still past kisses to outnumber
>   At tender eye-dawn of aurorean love:

The fact that they *are* immortal, indeed, brought home to us by the reference to 'their pinions' and the repetition of 'winged', contributes to the poet's surprise at finding them in this embrace. Their love would seem to be much the same thing as 'breathing human passion'. Yet there is a difference, for no trace of grossness or feverishness can be found in the lines. The associations of 'ready still past kisses to outnumber' are counterbalanced by 'calm-breathing', and the 'cool-rooted flowers', whose very colours add to the impression of coolness. The union of Eros and Psyche thus strikes one as being sensual and pure at the same time. This is what has come to the poet with the force of a revelation. Sexual love and spiritual values are no longer seen as incompatible, as though one had to be shame-faced about the first in presence of the other. The imagined vision of Eros and Psyche in the forest is Keats's way of telling us that he has come to this new realization. He is truly seeing both love and the spirit 'with *awaken'd* eyes', for he is now 'awake' to a reality that he had not glimpsed before.

We have still, however, to say what we mean by 'spiritual values'. The clue to this is the close association in the ode between Psyche and the business of poetic composition. The floral bed upon which the immortal lovers embrace in the first stanza finds both parallel and contrast in the sanctuary dedicated to the goddess which the last stanza describes:

> And in the midst of this wide quietness
> A rosy sanctuary will I dress
> With the wreath'd trellis of a working brain,
>   With buds, and bells, and stars without a name,
> With all the gardener Fancy e'er could feign,
>   Who breeding flowers, will never breed the same:

If the parallel is an obvious matter of using flowers in both passages, the contrast is far more subtle and important. The flowers of the last stanza are metaphorical 'flowers', products of the poet's '*working brain*', like the 'branched thoughts' mentioned earlier. The words 'wreath'd trellis', the rather awkward and 'tongue-twisting' articulation of which suggests the intricately twining flowers, also refer metaphorically to the densely intricate poetic texture which the 'working brain' of the literary artist brings into being. If the 'stars' are 'without a name', it is because they have never existed before. They are completely new creations of the poet's imagination, as are the flowers 'feigned' by 'the gardener Fancy'. The blooms in his garden are likewise bred from the 'working brain', and will never be 'the same' (i.e. 'repeated') because the fertile soil of poetic invention is perpetually bodying forth new thoughts and new images.

The two central stanzas complement one another. Superficially they appear extremely similar, as certain lines of each make use of almost exactly the same words in the same positions. But Keats is not breeding the same flowers in both stanzas. The repetition of the words emphasizes the essential difference in meaning between them.

Stanza II begins by singing the praises of Psyche in a formal, somewhat ritualistic style:

> O latest born and loveliest vision far
>   Of all Olympus' faded hierarchy!
> Fairer than Phoebe's sapphire-region'd star,
>   Or Vesper, amorous glow-worm of the sky;

The reference to 'Olympus' *faded* hierarchy' is echoed in stanza III, where Keats imagines Psyche's wings, her 'lucent fans', 'Fluttering among the *faint* Olympians'. The deities of Olympus are 'faded' and 'faint' because they are no more believed in —no more believed in, that is to say, as supernatural beings. 'Spiritual values' for Keats, whatever they may be, assuredly do not mean a return to Greek religion. He may feel a touch of regret that such a return is impossible, for stanza III speaks a little wistfully of the 'happy pieties' from which modern times are 'so far retir'd'. But he also implies, by referring to 'the fond believing lyre' of the ancient worshipper, that man has on the whole done well to shed his belief in the Olympians. Keats is no lover of superstition. 'Fond' can mean 'foolish' as well as 'devoted'. Yet the ancient deities may still be 'believed in' as enduring symbols of various aspects of human life. And for Keats, Psyche plainly has a very special significance.

The formal note on which the second stanza began grows

more pronounced in the remaining lines, with interestingly paradoxical effect:

> Fairer than these, though temple thou hast none,
> > Nor altar heap'd with flowers;
> Nor virgin-choir to make delicious moan
> > Upon the midnight hours;
> No voice, no lute, no pipe, no incense sweet
> > From chain-swung censer teeming;
> No shrine, no grove, no oracle, no heat
> > Of pale-mouth'd prophet dreaming.

As statement the lines mean that Psyche became a goddess too late to be worshipped like the older deities. Their tone of incantation, on the other hand, suggests the kind of ritual with which she was too late to be honoured.

In stanza III, whose last six lines largely repeat the words of the corresponding lines in stanza II, the ritualistic effect is put to most original use. Keats is explicit about the contrast between the age in which he is writing, and the time of 'antique vows'

> When holy were the haunted forest boughs,
> > Holy the air, the water, and the fire;

Despite man's altered beliefs, however, the poet says that he can 'see' Psyche, and sing her praises 'by my own eyes inspired'. He 'sees' her, not as a goddess to be worshipped, but as a symbol that beautifully embodies something profoundly important to him as a poet. His praise of her has nothing to do with the beliefs of antiquity. It is rather a matter of what she means symbolically to *him*. He therefore declares his desire and intention to give her, again symbolically, the 'vows' which she was too late to receive from antiquity itself:

> So let me be thy choir, and make a moan
> > Upon the midnight hours;
> Thy voice, thy lute, thy pipe, thy incense sweet
> > From swinged censer teeming;
> Thy shrine, thy grove, thy oracle, thy heat
> > Of pale-mouthed prophet dreaming.

The corresponding lines in the previous stanza have evoked the atmosphere of antique religion. In reproducing their pattern,

Keats gives it a completely different significance by making the whole ritual a creation, not of religion, *but of the poetic imagination*.

We are thus not surprised when poet takes the place of priest in the final stanza:

> Yes, I will be thy priest, and build a fane
> In some untrodden region of my mind,

The ritual apparatus will be as 'feigned' as are the flowers bred by 'the gardener Fancy'. We can now be in no doubt that the spiritual values associated with Psyche in this ode are the power and fertility of man's creative imagination, here represented specifically by the 'working brain' of the poet. Man's spirit, for Keats, is that in him which makes him 'build', which makes the 'branched thoughts' grow from his mind, which makes him impose order and harmony to achieve the 'wide quietness' in which his finest utterances may be heard.

There remain the last four lines:

> And there shall be for thee all soft delight
> That shadowy thought can win,
> A bright torch, and a casement ope at night,
> To let the warm Love in!

This conclusion expresses with remarkable concentration that reconciliation of love and spiritual values symbolized in the first stanza by the vision of Psyche and Eros embracing. Keats does not merely place the two things side by side, without conflict. Nor does he suggest that love should be ethereal and non-physical. The sensual reverberations of the final line are plain enough to counter any such notion. From the 'shadowy thought' of the poet, so described because it suggests the original obscurity and vagueness in the poet's mind before the bright image eventually issues from it, comes 'all soft delight'. This suggests downy 'luxury', yet it is meant for a personage who embodies spiritual values. If spiritual values *are* the poetic imagination, there can be no conflict between them and what springs out of that imagination. Thus the 'bright torch', guiding Love on his way to Psyche through the open casement, likewise originates, paradoxical though it may seem, in the realm of 'shadowy thought'.

The reader has already been warned not to expect a chronological treatment of the odes. In no sense can the *Ode to Psyche* be regarded as an 'advance' upon the odes previously considered. The point of considering it at this late stage of the discussion is simply that it represents a view of love and the spirit different from that of the *Ode on a Grecian Urn*, and conveniently examined after analysis of that poem. Keats is here certainly far from the mood of *La Belle Dame sans Merci*, the ballad-imitation in which a melancholy 'knight-at-arms' tells the story of his passion for a lady 'Full beautiful—a faery's child', and his subsequent horrifying dream when she has lulled him asleep:

> I saw pale kings and princes too,
>   Pale warriors, death-pale were they all;
> They cried—'La Belle Dame sans Merci
>   Hath thee in thrall!'
>
> I saw their starved lips in the gloam,
>   With horrid warning gaped wide,
> And I awoke and found me here,
>   On the cold hill's side.

The connection between that and the poet's feelings about 'breathing human passion' in the *Ode on a Grecian Urn* should be plain. But, quite apart from the unanswerable question of exactly when each poem started to germinate in the poet's mind, it would be unprofitable to view the differences and similarities between individual poems as representing a chronologically significant line of varying moods, whatever justification for this might be found in Keats's biography. All one can safely say is that in this year of extraordinary productiveness, Keats felt and thought in different ways at various different times, about things with which he had for long been preoccupied; and succeeded, through the power of his 'working brain', in making major poetry out of them. The poetry is major because of the intelligence with which the besetting tensions are grasped, the character with which they are faced, the subtlety with which their complexities are examined, and the linguistic vitality through which all this is bodied forth.

To Autumn is Keats's supreme triumph in the handling of poetic resources. To many readers it is the most satisfying of the odes for additional reasons. It contains no pronouncements, no overt statements of significance like 'She dwells with Beauty— Beauty that must die', no sense of obvious personal involvement. On the surface the ode might seem to be no more than a consummate piece of 'nature poetry', in which the sights, sounds, scents, and the very 'feel' of autumn are given to us in marvellously evocative language. That it does convey an impression of the season so vividly that a reader who has never lived in a temperate climate will know from the poem what autumn is like, is of course an important part of its distinction. Yet it does more, and does it without any hint of explicit 'preaching'.

Superficially altogether different from the *Ode on Melancholy*, *To Autumn* is profoundly related to that poem. As we have seen the *Melancholy* ode accepts the impermanence of beauty and joy as inevitable. Keats may not be particularly glad about this inevitability, but he does not cry out against it as he does in the *Ode to a Nightingale*, or, with far greater restraint, in the *Ode on a Grecian Urn*. *To Autumn* goes further. Here impermanence is accepted without the least trace of sadness, for the reason that Keats is able to see it as part of a larger and richer permanence.

This greater permanence is the continuity of life itself, in which the impermanence of the individual human existence is one tiny aspect of a vast and deathless pattern. The rotation of the seasons offers a symbol of this continuity that is immediately satisfying. Keats is nearest to explicit statement about the theme of his poem at the beginning of the last stanza, where for a few moments he wistfully recalls the sounds of a past season:

> Where are the songs of Spring? Ay, where are they?
> Think not of them, thou hast thy music too,

Though not explicit in pointing the parallel between the passing of the seasons and the transience of the individual human life, Keats is plain about the futility of regretting that spring has gone by. What is past is past. After all, autumn has its own characteristic sounds, which are as much part of the year as the 'songs of Spring'. Moreover, although autumn will be followed by the cold and barrenness of winter, winter will in turn give way to a fresh spring. Life goes on. The individual year may be drawing to its end, but there will be a new year to take its place. This is implicitly conveyed with wonderful effect in the very last line of the ode, 'And gathering swallows twitter in the skies'. In one way the line gives a premonition of the coming winter, for the swallows are gathering in preparation to migrate to warmer climes. Yet we remember that migratory birds return when the cold weather ends, so that the very hint of their impending departure carries with it an implied suggestion of their reappearance when warm days come again.

A converse effect is to be seen in the first line of the poem, 'Season of mists and mellow fruitfulness'. Since the overall impression made by the opening stanza is that of a steady, radiant warmth, the word 'mists' does not immediately suggest anything to the contrary. To one who knows the season of autumn in Europe, 'mists' will recall most obviously the haze experienced on a mellow day of sunshine, or the mist with which a warm autumn day may begin. But the very word 'mists' has among its associations a suggestion of chill, which hints, if only distantly, at the cold days of the coming winter, and death.

For the time being, however, all is richness and fruition. The season of autumn is like the full maturity of an individual man's life. It is therefore not surprising that Keats should use personification throughout the poem, as in the first stanza, where autumn is thought of as a person on terms of the warmest friendship with the very source of warmth itself:

> Close bosom-friend of the maturing sun;
> Conspiring with him how to load and bless
> With fruit the vines that round the thatch-eaves run;

'Conspiring' has in this context none of its customary sinister associations. Its effect is to add to the impression of warmth by intensifying the intimacy of the two bosom-friends. This conspiracy is a matter of two warm intimates benevolently putting their heads together to see how they can increase earth's glowing abundance. Keats deliberately employs the word 'maturing' in an ambiguous way. In one sense, 'maturing' refers to what the sun is actually doing, since its radiance is what brings the fruits of the earth to ripeness. But at the same time the sun can itself be regarded as undergoing a maturing process. It is like a fruit reaching final maturity, radiating a mellow glow which must soon be followed by the chill of winter, when all the fruits are picked and the harvest has been gathered in.

The last line quoted gives a fine example of Keats's use of language to enact meaning. The vine, which is a creeping plant, characteristically twines itself around the objects against which it grows, and here the movements made by the mouth of the reader in articulating words do actually suggest by analogy the twisting and twining growth of the plant round the overhanging projections of a thatched roof. We can see the same kind of thing going on in the next two lines:

> To bend with apples the moss'd cottage-trees,
> And fill all fruit with ripeness to the core;

The clear articulation of the language, especially 'moss'd cottage-trees' (the moss-grown apple-trees in a cottage garden), imposes a slow, heavy movement upon the reader. The heavy 'feel' of the words in the mouth is a physical analogy to the weight of apples richly loading the trees so that they bend beneath the strain.

As one would expect in a poem which contains such effects, the handling of verse-structure is wonderfully resourceful. Consider the use of the run-on line here:

> To swell the gourd, and plump the hazel shells
> With a sweet kernel; to set budding more,
> And still more, later flowers for the bees,
> Until they think warm days will never cease,
> For Summer has o'er-brimm'd their clammy cells.

If 'swell' and 'plump' give the outward signs of fat richness, the stress on 'sweet kernel', inevitable after the pause at the end of the previous line, vividly makes us think of the lusciousness within. And the imagined sweetness leads to the even greater sweetness of the honey made by the bees from their raids upon the flowers, whose seemingly endless budding is emphasized by the rhythm: 'to set budding more, And *still more*'. Once more, loaded abundance is suggested analogically by the heavy movement in the last line: 'o'er-brimm'd their clammy cells'. There is so much oozing sweetness here that the honeycombs are insufficient to hold it all.

Personification of autumn continues in the second stanza, where the season assumes the shape of people in various scenes typical of the season. The first four lines take us to a granary:

> Who hath not seen thee oft amid thy store?
> Sometimes whoever seeks abroad may find
> Thee sitting careless on a granary floor,
> Thy hair soft-lifted by the winnowing wind;

The function of 'careless' is to imply that the task of gathering in the harvest has been done and the storehouse has been filled. There is no more work to do. Notice how the sound of the soft wind of autumn is hinted at in the words '*winnow*ing *win*d'.

We then move to a cornfield, in which autumn appears as a slumbering reaper lying beside his half-finished furrow, his reaping hook inactive for the time being, and thus sparing, till he wakes, the next swath of corn and the flowers tangled in it:

> Or on a half-reap'd furrow sound asleep,
> Drowsed with the fume of poppies, while thy hook
> Spares the next swath and all its twined flowers;

The general heaviness of movement (consider the retarding effect of speaking 'a half-reap'd furrow' aloud) corresponds to the stupor of the slumbering man, whose 'Drowsed' condition is brought even more vividly home to us by the stress upon that word given to it by its place in the verse-structure. The awkward articulation of 'Spares the next swath and all its twined flowers', where the grouping of consonants prohibits easy flow, both contributes to the overall heaviness and works as an analogy, by way of sensation, to the tangle of flowers in among the corn.

The last four lines of the stanza afford equally fine instances of enactment. Autumn now figures as a gleaner, that is to say, a person who picks up the bits and pieces left behind in the reaped field when the crop has been carted away. He is visualized stepping across a small stream, his head loaded with his gatherings:

> And sometimes like a gleaner thou dost keep
> Steady thy laden head across a brook;
> Or by a cider-press, with patient look,
> Thou watchest the last oozings, hours by hours.

As F. R. Leavis has shown in his book *Revaluation*, Keats employs verse-structure here to enact the very movement of the gleaner. In the pause after 'keep', and the subsequent picking up of the sense with 'Steady', we have the prudent hesitation of the man carefully balancing his load before he crosses. And the step itself is enacted by the verbal step the reader makes when he moves from the last word of one line to the first word of the other, with the consciousness that the sense has been momentarily interrupted. In the last two lines, autumn takes the shape of the watcher by a cider-press, patiently waiting for the final trickles of juice from the crushed apples. Here the extreme slowness with which the drops issue from the press is suggested by 'watchest the last oozings, hours by hours'.

The concluding stanza, as we have seen, opens by briefly recalling the past, but goes on to dismiss regrets for the departed spring as merely vain, as autumn has its own 'music'. We have already commented on the contribution made to this 'music' by the 'gathering swallows'. Two other sounds call for special mention:

> Then in a wailful choir the small gnats mourn
> Among the river sallows, borne aloft
> Or sinking as the light wind lives or dies;
> And full-grown lambs loud bleat from hilly bourn;

'Wailful choir' and 'mourn', while deftly characterizing the thin noise made by a cloud of gnats, cannot help also linking their sound with the idea of a funeral dirge for the dying year. It is true that the year is still very much alive, yet the hint of death is impossible to miss. At the same time, the varying power of the 'light wind', sometimes living, sometimes dying, suggests the particular position of autumn, poised between the brilliant 'life' of summer and the 'death' of winter. Full maturity, after all, means that youth has been left far behind. The bleating heard 'from hilly bourn' is made by '*full-grown* lambs'. Observe the manner in which the transition from the second line of the passage to the third simultaneously conveys the impression of rising and falling, and, by momentarily leaving the sense suspended, gives the effect of poise between two alternatives analogous to autumn's crucial position in the cycle of seasons.

There are other hints of death in the stanza, for the sound of the gnats is heard

> While barred clouds bloom the soft-dying day,
> And touch the stubble-plains with rosy hue;

Yet the idea of death is not treated with horror or resentment. The day is dying *softly*, the rosy 'bloom' of sunset taking away from the stark bareness of the now fully reaped cornfields. And in any case, the very reference to the close of day, like the final line about the swallows, carries with it a suggestion of its opposite. Just as the swallows will come back next year, so another day will dawn, for the great movement of life goes on, however transient the existence of the individual.

6

'HYPERION'; THE TWO FRAGMENTS

Begun in December 1818, and abandoned in September of the following year, *Hyperion* is Keats's attempt to write an epic poem in the manner of Milton. His reasons for dropping the work are well known. 'I have given up *Hyperion*,' says one of his letters, '—there were too many Miltonic inversions in it—Miltonic verse cannot be written but in an artful, or rather, artist's humour. I wish to give myself up to other sensations. English ought to be kept up.' He did not wish the fragment to be printed, although it appeared in the volume of 1820 at the particular request of the publishers.

Hyperion is related to the *Ode to Psyche* in seeking to give a new value and relevance to Greek myth. Unlike the ode, however, *Hyperion* is not among Keats's happier performances. The mythological significance of the work is not embodied in poetry of sufficiently compelling quality to make it carry any great conviction. Whereas Keats's rediscovery of Psyche is also a rediscovery of himself as a poet, *Hyperion*, which might superficially strike the reader as being much the same thing, is for the most part a series of large but somewhat ineffectual gestures. Apollo may discover himself, from the angle of *story*, in the last lines of the fragment. The *poetry*, on the other hand, remains on the whole frigid, and quite without that feeling for the possibilities of language manifest in the odes.

Unsatisfactory though the work may be, it has considerable importance as what might be termed a 'line of transmission' for a combination of two major influences on later nineteenth-century English poetry. The essential points can be made conveniently from a glance at the opening lines:

> Deep in the shady sadness of a vale
> Far sunken from the healthy breath of morn,
> Far from the fiery noon, and eve's one star,
> Sat gray-hair'd Saturn, quiet as a stone,

Still as the silence round about his lair;
Forest on forest hung about his head
Like cloud on cloud. No stir of air was there,
Not so much life as on a summer's day
Robs not one light seed from the feather'd grass,
But where the dead leaf fell, there did it rest.
A stream went voiceless by, still deadened more
By reason of his fallen divinity
Spreading a shade: the Naiad 'mid her reeds
Press'd her cold finger closer to her lips.

Little comment is needed on the Miltonic aspect of the passage. Comparison with almost any tranquilly descriptive section of *Paradise Lost* will indicate the general similarity, which resides mainly in the gait of the verse. Keats's highly deliberate varying of the position of the caesura, especially obvious in the last eight lines, is the clearest evidence of Miltonic derivation. Yet the reader will probably feel that Milton is not the only presence here; and in trying to account for this impression, he may well say that Milton is characteristically far more robust. Consider the sentence 'No stir of air was there'. With its excessively contrived exploitation of vowel-sounds, it reads almost like an elocution exercise of the 'How now, brown cow' variety. It draws so much attention to itself that it risks awakening amusement. Certainly it is dangerously easy to parody.

Speaking more seriously, one is vividly reminded here of a line from the youthful *Epistle to Charles Cowden Clarke*— 'Spenserian vowels that elope with ease'. The old Spenserian influence, however, manifests itself now far more in a pre-occupation with verbal 'melody' than in a concern for gorgeous tapestry-weaving. Moreover, it is no accident that the line quoted appears in the following context:

Spenserian vowels that elope with ease,
And float along like birds o'er summer seas;
Miltonian storms, and more, Miltonian tenderness;
Michael in arms, and more, meek Eve's fair slenderness

Hyperion gives us a blend of Spenser and Milton—or, to put the matter more suggestively, it gives us Milton 'felt through' Spenser. The blend is hardly an eccentric one. Did not Milton himself admire Spenser as England's 'sage and serious poet'? Furthermore, the slight decorative charm of Milton's pastoral poetry is derived from Spenser.

What is most important from our point of view, however, is that the Spenser–Milton blend became something of an accepted norm for distinguishing what was regarded as being 'poetic'. The later nineteenth century, of course, is the Victorian Age, and in that period the dominant poetic figure is Tennyson. It is a commonplace that Keats is the major influence on Tennyson's early work. At times this influence stems from Keats's strength, as in *Mariana*, where such a line as 'The cluster'd marish mosses crept' exhibits the same power of rendering meaning through oral sensation that we find in the *Autumn* ode. (The clustering consonants parallel the clustered mosses.) On the whole, nevertheless, the side of Keats which most affects the early Tennyson is the decorative Spenserian side, as we see most plainly in the fanciful gorgeousness of *Recollections of the Arabian Nights*. Spenser apprehended by way of Keats is also the presence behind a much more mature poem, *The Lotos-Eaters*, where the use of the Spenserian stanza in the first part, not to mention actual echoes of *The Faerie Queene* later on, go with a pervasive narcotic 'luxury' decidedly reminiscent of the weaker Keats:

> The charmed sunset linger'd low adown
> In the red West: thro' mountain clefts the dale
> Was seen far inland, and the yellow down
> Border'd with palm, and many a winding vale
> And meadow, set with slender galingale;
> A land where all things always seem'd the same!
> And round about the keel with faces pale,
> Dark faces pale against that rosy flame,
> The mild-eyed melancholy Lotos-eaters came.

In a way such poetry can be called 'sensuous', in that it encourages the visualization of colour. Yet it is far removed from the sensuousness of the *Autumn* ode, where to think of the sensuous is to think, as happens so often in Shakespeare, of *sensation*. Tennyson, like Keats in most of his early work, offers merely a visual and aural 'glamour'—superbly contrived, no doubt, but weaker in its impact than the sensuousness which makes the reader taste the meaning on his palate, as it were. Keats's image of the bursting of joy's grape actually suggests the way in which much of his finest poetry works, the idea of joy being turned into vivid sensation. The stanza from *The Lotos-Eaters* draws most of its distinction from something else extremely different from the finest Keats—the highly calculated *smoothness* of its verse. Contrasted reading aloud of that stanza and any part of the *Autumn* ode will clearly reveal this. Tennyson has copied Spenser in choosing his words in such a way that the jolts and jars to which the English language is prone are made to seem almost non-existent. The Keats of *Hyperion* has much the same ambition. Compare 'No stir of air was there' with 'A land where all things always seem'd the same'. Different in immediate effect, the two examples none the less resemble each other in aiming at an impression of suave mellifluousness.

For the blend of Spenser and Milton which Keats transmitted through *Hyperion*, one should turn to the beginning of Tennyson's *Oenone*:

> There lies a vale in Ida, lovelier
> Than all the valleys of Ionian hills.
> The swimming vapour slopes athwart the glen,
> Puts forth an arm, and creeps from pine to pine,
> And loiters, slowly drawn. On either hand
> The lawns and meadow-ledges midway down
> Hang rich in flowers, and far below them roars
> The long brook falling thro' the clov'n ravine
> In cataract after cataract to the sea.
> Behind the valley topmost Gargarus
> Stands up and takes the morning: but in front
> The gorges, opening wide apart, reveal
> Troas and Ilion's column'd citadel,
> The crown of Troas.

No one can deny the consummate skill of that verse. Its effects of enactment, as when the sense is made to 'hang' like the 'lawns and meadow-ledges', though perhaps rather over-obvious, are thoroughly accomplished. The blend of Miltonic sonority (exemplified by 'cataract after cataract to the sea', and the studied use of proper names) with Spenserian smoothness ('And loiters, slowly drawn') is a complete success.

Of such verse, whatever its limitations, Tennyson is a real master. Keats, although he is the major immediate influence behind *Oenone*, can hardly be called the same. Contrived melli-fluousness is alien to his genius, which actually revels in the tough awkwardness of articulation so often imposed by the English language. 'English ought to be kept up.'

As one would expect from a poet so long under the fascination of Spenser, little though that spell has to do with his very best work, the more satisfactory parts of *Hyperion* are those, such as the opening, in which the Spenserian aspect of the blend is most to the fore. The obviously Miltonic passages, aiming at an epic grandeur and largeness of conception, are often unfortunate. A fair example is the description of Thea, beginning at line 26:

> She was a Goddess of the infant world;
> By her in stature the tall Amazon
> Had stood a pigmy's height: she would have ta'en
> Achilles by the hair and bent his neck;
> Or with a finger stay'd Ixion's wheel.
> Her face was large as that of Memphian sphinx,
> Pedestal'd haply in a palace-court,
> When sages look'd to Egypt for their lore.

Granted that Keats is writing about the Titans, whose fall at the hands of a new race of deities provides the background of the poem, the emphasis upon the sheer size of the goddess is gro-tesque, and perilously close to comedy. Milton has far subtler ways of suggesting the dimensions of Satan in *Paradise Lost*. Equally unhappy are what are intended to be the great dramatic 'moments', like the beginning of Hyperion's first speech:

> 'O dreams of day and night!
> O monstrous forms! O effigies of pain!
> O spectres busy in a cold, cold gloom!
> O lank-ear'd Phantoms of black-weeded pools!
> Why do I know ye? why have I seen ye? why
> Is my eternal essence thus distraught
> To see and to behold these horrors new?'

The lines are no more than a series of ejaculations, aiming at rhetorical power, but achieving only empty bombast.

The Fall of Hyperion, Keats's unfinished attempt to revise the other poem in a manner congenial to him, is among his most impressive works. His determination to keep clear of the Spenserian–Miltonic mode is evident again and again in the lines that he actually recast. 'No stir of air was there', for instance, becomes 'No stir of life Was in this shrouded vale'. But the real interest of the work lies in the totally new material that it introduces, above all the vision of Moneta.

The narrative begins against a background which suggests richness and abundance of life and growth:

> Methought I stood where trees of every clime,
> Palm, myrtle, oak, and sycamore, and beech,
> With plantane and spice-blossoms, made a screen,
> In neighbourhood of fountains (by the noise
> Soft-showering in mine ears), and (by the touch
> Of scent) not far from roses.

In the midst of this profusion, the poet finds what appears to be 'a feast of summer fruits', spread on a mound before the entrance to an arbour. He partakes, not only of the food, but of the refreshment offered by 'a cool vessel of transparent juice', which plunges him into deep slumber. It is essential to realize that this is not a heart-easing sleep into which the poet sinks gratefully, for he struggles hard against it. The 'domineering potion', indeed, removes him from the rich abundance he has been enjoying. When he wakes, the whole scene has changed:

> the fair trees were gone,
> The mossy mound and arbour were no more:
> I look'd around upon the carved sides
> Of an old sanctuary, with roof august,
> Builded so high, it seem'd that filmed clouds
> Might spread beneath as o'er the stars of heaven.
> So old the place was, I remember'd none
> The like upon the earth:

The change from the gracious profusion of the first scene to this awe-inspiring sight hints at disconcerting experiences to come.

Comfort and security have been left behind with the 'fair trees', through the agency of the treacherous juice.

The poet's feet are as though irresistibly impelled towards the dominating feature of the scene,

> An image, huge of feature as a cloud,
> At level of whose feet an altar slept,
> To be approach'd on either side by steps
> And marble balustrade, and patient travail
> To count with toil the innumerable degrees.

Notice the manner in which the verse-movement already suggests the imagined weary labour of climbing the steps. Its effect is prophetic, for a voice commands the poet to ascend the steps and gain the top before the 'gummed leaves' fragrantly burning in the shrine are consumed. If he fails to do this, he must die. So there ensues what is symbolically a desperate race with death. The difficulty of movement is conveyed to us by the verse with all the agony of nightmare:

> I strove hard to escape
> The numbness, strove to gain the lowest step.
> Slow, heavy, deadly was my pace: the cold
> Grew stifling, suffocating, at the heart;
> And when I clasp'd my hands I felt them not.
> One minute before death my iced foot touch'd
> The lowest stair;

Once on the lowest step he is reprieved from the death sentence, and he mounts without labour. The 'veiled shadow' at the summit tells him the significance of what has just happened:

> Thou hast felt
> What 'tis to die and live again before
> Thy fated hour;

Pressed for more enlightenment about the place and why the poet is there, she answers that 'None can usurp this height . . .

> But those to whom the miseries of the world
> Are misery, and will not let them rest.'

But the poet cannot understand why he does not see other men there; for surely he is not alone in feeling 'the giant agony of the world'. Moneta (as she later reveals herself to be) replies that he is distinguished from them by being a 'dreamer', a visionary. This confers no superiority upon him, however, for the 'dreaming thing' is a weaker creature than those who

> seek no wonder but the human face,
> No music but a happy-noted voice:
> They come not here, they have no thought to come;
> And thou art here, for thou art less than they.
> What benefit canst thou, or all thy tribe,
> To the great world?

Yet there can be pity for the dreamer, who 'venoms all his days, Bearing more woe than all his sins deserve'. It is because of this that men such as he are 'admitted oft' to glimpses of happiness symbolized by the gardens from which the 'domineering potion' has carried him away.

The poet must know more, for there is within him a nagging anxiety about his own identity. Surely poetry itself is not useless and contemptible, even if he cannot truly call himself a poet. She has spoken of his 'tribe'. What exactly has she meant? Moneta answers by repeating that he is a dreamer, and, what is most important, emphasizes that poet and dreamer are utterly distinct from one another:

> 'Art not thou of the dreamer tribe?
> The poet and the dreamer are distinct,
> Diverse, sheer opposite, antipodes,
> The one pours out a balm upon the world,
> The other vexes it.'

Although one of those who feel 'the miseries of the world', he is also, paradoxically, one who actually adds to them.

For his 'good will', however, he will be vouchsafed a vision of the scenes still vividly present in Moneta's brain—scenes which would have told the tale, had the poem been finished, of the fall of Hyperion. With what exists of these scenes we are not concerned. The climax of the fragment, and its most impressive poetry, come before the narrative proper begins. The poet is filled with

wonder at the soft tenderness of Moneta's speech, yet is fearful of
her at the same time:

> And yet I had a terror of her robes,
> And chiefly of the veils from her brow
> Hung pale, and curtain'd her in mysteries,
> That made my heart too small to hold its blood.
> This saw that Goddess, and with sacred hand
> Parted the veils.

And there follows the vision of Moneta's face in the passage we
quoted in chapter 1.

What is the significance of this vision? We may best define
it by returning to the paradoxes noted in our earlier discussion
of the passage. In their context, as we saw, the words 'bright'
and immortal' have a disturbing impact which cannot be
explained away by pointing to their purely literal meaning. We
have seen something like this happening elsewhere in Keats,
notably in the *Ode on Melancholy*, where the evocation of
apparently contradictory associations contributes to a subtler
'meaning' that cannot be conveyed in terms of statement. The
refreshing of the 'droop-headed flowers' in stanza two of the ode,
we remember, is one of the ways in which Keats communicates
his sense of the mingling of the pleasurable and the painful in
human existence. Now, although the painful is well to the fore in
the vision of Moneta, one would hardly regard the pleasurable
as being an ingredient of these lines! At the same time, however,
Keats does wish the reader to feel the powerfully different
impressions made by Moneta upon the awe-struck beholder.
She is both tender and frightening, serene in her sad authority
and also profoundly disquieting. 'Not pined by human sorrows',
she yet stands as an embodiment of the very idea of sorrow
itself, at an 'immortal' level far above the incidental sorrows
of the individual human being. The oddly disturbing words
are therefore employed as a means of making us realize the
strange, majestic apartness of Moneta. Through the paradoxical
associations which they conjure up, they bring to the reader
a sense of her mystery, where desolate aloofness mingles with a
benign compassion.

Moneta, indeed, embodies a kind of 'permanence' less consoling than the view presented by the *Autumn* ode—the permanence of suffering. But it would not be correct to regard *The Fall of Hyperion* as an essentially depressing poem. In point of fact, the inadequate poetry of the earlier fragment, by contrast with the spareness and tautness of the *Fall*, is infinitely more 'depressing' in effect. *The Fall of Hyperion* is no more conventionally depressing than a Shakespeare tragedy, to say which is really to put one's finger upon the nature of the poem. For it is 'tragic' in the deepest sense, and Keats's own words suggest that he was fully aware of this. The 'dreamer' of the poem tells how

> at the view of sad Moneta's brow,
> I ask'd to see what things the hollow brain
> Behind environ'd: what high tragedy
> In the dark secret chambers of her skull
> Was acting, that could give so dread a stress
> To her cold lips, and fill with such a light
> Her planetary eyes, and touch her voice
> With such a sorrow.

The poem is supremely tragic because it reaches the profound impersonality of tragedy. In fact, the whole progress of the 'action', from its opening in the lush gardens, through the desperate race with the burning leaves, to the encounter with Moneta culminating in the vision of her face, is like a miniature allegory of the artist's attainment of that impersonality. From initial comfort and well-being, he passes through acute personal anguish to deep self-questioning, symbolized by the dialogue with Moneta concerning his identity, and finally reaches that sense of 'impersonal' sorrow embodied in Moneta's face— 'impersonal' because it transcends the individual sufferer. And in the confrontation of this impersonal sorrow there is a strange serenity, of which the symbol is the 'benignant light' of Moneta's eyes.

7

THE LETTERS

Keats's letters are, in their own way, a classic work of English literature. To start thus with a truism, once again, is a means towards attempting definition—definition, in this case, of just what it is that gives these writings their peculiar status. The description of them as a 'work' of literature is, of course, technically incorrect. A 'work' suggests the outcome of conscious application, something that has been literally 'worked at', like Keats's own *Ode to Psyche*. With the exception of the verse epistles, Keats's letters were written simply *as* letters, not as works of art. Yet to go through this miscellaneous collection, addressed almost entirely to the friends and close relatives whose regard and affection the poet valued so highly, is, for many readers, to experience a sense of extraordinary unity in what may at first seem to be quite heterogeneous material.

If it is this sense of unity that makes the term 'work', though technically inaccurate, at least not altogether inappropriate, we are naturally impelled to seek reasons for it. Part of the explanation is that these letters are the vivid expression of a lively and distinctive personality, whose humour, sensitivity and penetration dominate the collection up to the brief and bitter exhaustion of the final phase. Keats's sense of humour shows itself again and again in a wonderfully zestful feeling for the ridiculous, as in the account of 'a private theatrical' in Letter 41:

—I left off short in my last, just as I began an account of a private theatrical—Well it was of the lowest order, all greasy and oily, insomuch that if they had lived in olden times, when signs were hung over the doors; the only appropriate one for that oily place would have been—a guttered Candle—They played John Bull, The Review—and it was to conclude with Bombastes Furioso—I saw from a Box the 1st Act of John Bull, then I went to Drury and did not return till it was over—when by Wells's interest we got behind the scenes—there was not a yard wide all the way round for actors, scene-shifters and interlopers to move in; for 'Nota Bene' the Green Room was under the stage and there was I threatened over and over again to be turned out by the oily scene-shifters—There did K hear a little painted Trollop own, very candidly, that she had failed in Mary, with a 'damned if she'd play a serious part again, as long as she lived', and at the same time she was habited as the Quaker in the Review—There was a quarrel, and a fat good-natured looking girl in soldiers' Clothes wished she had only been a man for Tom's sake—One fellow began a song, but an unlucky finger-point from the Gallery sent him off like a shot. One chap was dressed to kill for the King in Bombastes, and he stood at the edge of the scene in the very sweat of anxiety to show himself, but alas the thing was not played. The sweetest morsel of the night moreover was, that the Musicians began pegging and fagging away at an overture—never did you see faces more in earnest, three times did they play it over, dropping all kinds of correctness and still did not the curtain draw up—

Earlier in the same letter, however, we find this, so very different in tone and interest, yet equally characteristic:

I think a little change has taken place in my intellect lately—I cannot bear to be uninterested or unemployed, I, who for so long a time have been addicted to passiveness. Nothing is finer for the purposes of great productions than a very gradual ripening of the intellectual powers. As an instance of this observe—I sat down yesterday to read 'King Lear' once again the thing appeared to demand the prologue of a Sonnet, I wrote it and began to read—(I know you would like to see it.)

And Keats transcribes the new poem, 'On sitting down to read King Lear once again', after which he remarks, 'So you see I am getting at it, with a sort of determination and strength.'

'*Getting at it*'—here in those three words is the supreme reason why the letters impress us with a sense of unity. For no matter how far Keats's zest for the absurd, or his sensitivity to the feelings of others, or his frequent if sometimes tardy penetration into human character, may seem to carry him from the art of poetry as such, these things are part and parcel of the developing poet. The often vivid descriptions of natural scenery in the letters have an evident connection with much in the poetry: 'The Approach to Loch Awe was very solemn towards nightfall—

the first glance was a streak of water deep in the Bases of large black mountains—'(Letter 78). The same may be said of the ways in which sense-impressions are recorded: 'Devonshire continues! rainy. As the drops beat against the window, they give me the same sensation as a quart of cold water offered to revive a half-drowned devil—No feel of the clouds dropping fatness; *but as if the roots of the Earth were rotten cold and drench'd*—' (Letter 60. My italics). But Keats's reactions to things not obviously 'poetic', like the private theatrical, are by no means irrelevant. A very young man, he is urgently striving towards maturity as an artist, and every kind of experience has its place in the total maturing process out of which man and artist take shape.

If much the same thing can doubtless be said to some extent about any writer of distinction, it has especial point in the case of Keats. For what dominates the letters is his determination to grasp experience as fully as possible, to make himself into the kind of man and artist he wishes to be. '*Getting at it*' for Keats thus means more than merely sitting down to write; it involves a strenuous effort of the intelligence, an intense will to develop, and a rapid growth in his ability to make important discriminations with regard both to his own work and that of others. Our consideration of the letters will accordingly concentrate on passages which relate specifically to Keats's ideas about his own business as a practising poet, and about literature in general, but the reader should be warned against forgetting the significance of other passages that have no immediately obvious bearing upon the poetry. Keats's walking-tour in Northern England and Scotland, for example, quite apart from the actual pieces of verse contained in the letters describing it, must be seen as the poet himself saw it—as a planned part of his development:

I purpose within a Month to put my knapsack at my back and make a pedestrian tour through the North of England, and part of Scotland—to make a sort of Prologue to the Life I intend to pursue—that is to write, to study and to see all Europe at the lowest expence. I will clamber through the Clouds and exist.

From the earliest letters we are aware of Keats's absorption in the very thought of poetry, and his feeling of responsibility as an artist. The recollection of two lines from Shakespeare leads him on to say

I find that I cannot exist without poetry—without eternal poetry—half the day will not do—the whole of it—I began with a little, but habit has made me a Leviathan—I had become all in a tremble from not having written any thing of late—the Sonnet over leaf did me some good. I slept the better last night for it—this Morning, however, I am nearly as bad again—. (Letter 13.)

And in Letter 14 he writes, 'I went to the Isle of Wight—thought so much about Poetry so long together that I could not get to sleep at night.' If that may perhaps strike the reader as little more than boyishly excited enthusiasm, he must be reminded that even at this stage Keats in no way underestimates the hard work and self-discipline involved in being a poet of any substance:

I have asked myself so often why I should be a Poet more than other Men,—seeing how great a thing it is,—how great things are to be gained by it—What a thing to be in the Mouth of Fame—that at last the Idea has grown so monstrously beyond my seeming Power of attainment that the other day I nearly consented with myself to drop into a Phaeton—yet 'tis a disgrace to fail even in a huge attempt, and at this moment I drive the thought from me. I began my Poem about a Fortnight since and have done some every day except travelling ones—Perhaps I may have done a good deal for the time but it appears such a Pin's Point to me that I will not coppy any out. When I consider that so many of these Pin points go to form a Bodkin point (God send I end not my Life with a bare Bodkin, in its modern sense) and that it requires a thousand bodkins to make a Spear bright enough to throw any light to posterity—I see that nothing but continual uphill Journeying.! (Letter 14.)

In Letter 15 he tells Benjamin Robert Haydon, 'I have been in such a state of mind as to read over my Lines and hate them. I am "one that gathers Samphire dreadful trade" the Cliff of Poesy Towers above me . . .' At the same time he is determined to persist, his 'occasional depressions' notwithstanding: 'However I must think that difficulties nerve the Spirit of a Man—they make our Prime Objects a Refuge as well as a Passion.' And

Letter 15 also shows us Keats's intelligent and far from boyish awareness of the dangers of self-delusion:

There is no greater Sin after the 7 deadly than to flatter oneself into an idea of being a great Poet—or one of those beings who are privileged to wear out their Lives in the pursuit of Honor—how comfortable a feel it is that such a Crime must bring its heavy Penalty? That if one be a Selfdeluder accounts will be balanced?

Nothing, indeed, could be more remote from self-delusion than Keats's view of *Endymion*, his first long sustained effort of creation. We have already seen what he says of that poem in his astonishingly candid Preface. Compare the Preface with this passage from Letter 25, written when the work was still incomplete:

You will be glad to hear that within these last three weeks I have written 1000 lines—which are the third Book of my Poem. My Ideas with respect to it I assure you are very low—and I would write the subject thoroughly again—but I am tired of it and think the time would be better spent in writing a new Romance which I have in my eye for next Summer—Rome was not built in a Day—and all the good I expect from my employment this summer is the fruit of Experience which I hope to gather in my next Poem.

Thus, whilst abundantly aware of the shortcomings of the poem, Keats clearly recognizes the value of having written it. We cannot be surprised at the severity of the Preface, for Keats has left the *Endymion* phase of his development behind before the work is even finished. In his eyes the poem is of little or no worth as an achievement; its value lies in what it has taught him about being a poet. He is therefore far from pained or shocked when he reads a letter in the *Morning Chronicle* of 3 October 1818 signed 'J.S.', friendly to the poem on the whole, yet asserting that, in view of its weaknesses, 'a real friend of the author would have dissuaded him from an immediate publication':

... I begin to get a little acquainted with my own strength and weakness.—Praise or blame has put a momentary effect on the man whose love of beauty in the abstract makes him a severe critic on his own Works. My own domestic criticism has given me pain without comparison beyond what Blackwood or the Quarterly could possibly inflict, and also when I feel I am right, no external praise can give me such a glow as my own solitary reperception & ratification of what is fine. J.S. is perfectly right in regard to the slip-shod Endymion. That it is so is no fault of mine.—No!—though it may sound a little paradoxical. It is as good as I had power to make it—by myself. Had I been nervous about its being a perfect piece, & with that view asked advice, & trembled over every page, it would not have been written; for it is not in my nature to fumble—I will write independently.—I have written independently *without Judgment*.—I may write independently, & *with Judgment* hereafter. The Genius of Poetry must work out its own salvation in a man: It cannot be matured by law and precept, but by sensation & watchfulness in itself. That which is creative must create itself—In Endymion, I leaped headlong into the Sea, and thereby have become better acquainted with the Soundings, the quicksands, & the rocks, than if I had stayed upon the green shore, and piped a silly pipe, and took tea & comfortable advice.—I was never afraid of failure; for I would sooner fail than not be among the greatest. (Letter 90.)

The maturity of attitude which makes his own strictures far more damaging than those of hostile reviewers, the clear insight into the nature of his creative processes, the concentrated power of expression, which impress the reader of Letter 90, are themselves the best possible proof of the distance Keats has travelled since he embarked upon *Endymion*. This development in his own artistic powers, which is also a development of character and intelligence, is paralleled by a progressive deepening of penetration into other writers. In this connection it is illuminating to glance at some of his observations on a great contemporary, Wordsworth.

Keats is certainly not lacking in respect for Wordsworth. Indeed, all his comments upon him are based on the assumption that he is a great poet. But this does not preclude a lively awareness of Wordsworth's weak points, nor does it prevent Keats from making fun of his absurdities. Letter 23 is a good example of this, on the level of pure burlesque:

... Wordsworth sometimes, though in a fine way, gives us sentences in the style of school exercises—For instance,

> The lake doth glitter
> Small birds twitter &c.

Now, I think this is an excellent method of giving a very clear description of an interesting place such as Oxford is—

Whereupon he launches into a exuberant parody:

> The Gothic looks solemn—
> The plain Doric column
> Supports an old Bishop & Crosier;
> The mouldering arch,
> Shaded o'er by a larch,
> Lives next door to Wilson the Hosier

(It is worth pointing out that in Letter 22, addressed to the same correspondent, Keats copies out a poem by the seventeenth-century poetess Katherine Philips, enthusiastically commending it to his friend's attention. That he should have perceived the quality of a metaphysical poem of this type, so very different from the poetry of his age, is itself indicative of the subtlety of mind and feeling that later produced the great odes.)

Letter 44, though again exhibiting the writer's characteristic wit, contains thoughtful and substantial criticism. 'It may be said', Keats remarks, 'that we ought to read our Contemporaries —that Wordsworth &c. should have their due from us. But, for the sake of a few fine imaginative or domestic passages, are we to be bullied into a certain Philosophy engendered in the whims of an Egotist—.' It is the sheer obtrusiveness of the Wordsworthian philosophy, and that of other poets who seem to insist that the reader should think the way they do, that irritates Keats. Why, he asks, should one man suppose that his ideas are of such over-whelming importance? 'Every man has his speculations, but every man does not brood and peacock over them till he makes a false coinage and deceives himself.' When a poet harps too much on his way of seeing things, the reader justifiably resists, for 'We hate poetry that has a palpable design upon us—and if we do not agree, seems to put its hand in its breeches pocket. Poetry should be great and unobtrusive . . .' To Keats the poetry of the Eliza-bethan age has this quality of unobtrusiveness, an unobtrusive-ness like that of such familiar objects as flowers. 'How beautiful are the retired flowers! how would they lose their beauty were they to throng into the highway crying out, "admire me I am a violet!—dote upon me I am a primrose!"' Keats is not saying that Wordsworth, or even Leigh Hunt, are valueless: he is simply exasperated by their 'palpable design' upon the reader, which is something that the Elizabethans did so well without. '—I don't mean to deny Wordsworth's grandeur and Hunt's merit, but I mean to say we need not be teazed with grandeur and merit when we can have them uncontaminated and unobtrusive. Let us have the old Poets . . .'

Letter 50 draws an explicit distinction between Wordsworth the poet and Wordsworth the would-be philosopher: 'I am sorry that Wordsworth has left a bad impression where-ever he visited in town by his egotism, Vanity, and bigotry. Yet he is a great poet if not a philosopher.' Without the irritated mood and rather wholesale approach of Letter 44, Keats is here making the same distinction later arrived at by Matthew Arnold between the 'reality' of Wordsworth's poetry, and the 'illusion' of his philosophy. When we reach Letter 64, however, we find a far deeper and more complex response to Wordsworth, which reveals a deepening response to life itself. Endeavouring to define the nature of Wordsworth's genius, Keats proposes an analogy:

—I compare human life to a large Mansion of Many Apartments, two of which I can only describe, the doors of the rest being as yet shut upon me. The first we step into we call the infant or thoughtless Chamber, in which we remain as long as we do not think—We remain there a long while, and notwithstanding the doors of the second Chamber remain wide open, showing a bright appearance, we care not to hasten to it; but are at length imperceptibily impelled by the awakening of this thinking principle within us—we no sooner get into the second Chamber, which I shall call the Chamber of Maiden-Thought, than we become intoxicated with the light and the atmosphere, we see nothing but pleasant wonders, and think of delaying there for ever in delight: However among the effects this breathing is father of is that tremendous one of sharpening one's vision into the heart and nature of Man—of convincing one's nerves that the world is full of Misery and Heartbreak, Pain, Sickness and oppression—whereby this Chamber of Maiden Thought becomes gradually darkened and at the same time on all sides of it many doors are set open—but all dark—all leading to dark passages—We see not the ballance of good and evil. We are in a Mist. *We* are now in that state—We feel the 'burden of the Mystery' . . .

If the process described as taking place in the 'Chamber of Maiden Thought' recalls the transition from the 'joys' of *Sleep and Poetry* to 'the agonies, the strife Of human hearts', there are important differences to be noted. *Sleep and Poetry* shows Keats passing from one phase of existence, the phase associated with 'luxury', to 'a nobler life'. There can be no mistake about the poet's intention, whether it is realized or not, to turn his back upon the pleasures of the earlier phase and adopt a new and serious attitude to living. But in Letter 64, Keats sees the 'joys' ('we become intoxicated with the light and the atmosphere, we see nothing but pleasant wonders, and think of delaying there for ever in delight') and the vision of 'the agonies, the strife Of human hearts', as belonging to the same phase of existence ('convincing one's nerves that the world is full of Misery and Heartbreak, Pain, Sickness and oppression'). That is to say, instead of regarding the awareness of human suffering as simply antithetical to the 'joys' to which he bids farewell in *Sleep and Poetry*, Keats here views that awareness as emerging from the very process that has enabled the 'joys' to be savoured.

The awareness, however, is not immediately complete, for it takes time to convince one's nerves of the reality of human misery, not to mention its extent. One does not grow into a wholly mature person overnight, as it were. Indeed, the question of the *extent* of man's suffering is at this stage particularly baffling—'We see not the ballance of good and evil.' Where does the one end and the other begin? How much good is there for all the evil that exists in the world? We cannot say, for as yet 'We are in a mist'.

It is from this view of human development, so much more adequate than the relatively facile approach of *Sleep and Poetry*, that Keats proceeds to his definition of Wordsworth's genius:

We feel 'the burden of the Mystery', to this Point was Wordsworth come, as far as I can perceive when he wrote 'Tintern Abbey' and it seems to me that his Genius is explorative of those dark Passages. Now if we live, and go on thinking, we too shall explore them—he is a Genius and superior to us, in so far as he can, more than we, make discoveries, and shed a light in them—Here I must think Wordsworth is deeper than Milton—

And he goes on to a comparative discussion of the two poets, which, whether one agrees with its conclusions or not, reveals a most striking critical and historical sense. What stands out quite plainly is that Keats's previous separation of Wordsworth the poet from Wordsworth the philosopher will no longer do. Keats, after all, is fundamentally right. The distinction may be justifiable in talking about Wordsworth's inferior work, or even in connection with unsuccessful passages in the major poems; but as far as his very finest poetry is concerned, it is dubious, to say the least. In Letter 93, Keats hits upon a happy formula for describing the Wordsworthian 'poetical Character'. Explicitly distinguishing it from that of other poets, he calls this 'poetical Character' the 'egotistical sublime; which is a thing per se and stands alone'. Here Keats's earlier exasperation at Wordsworth's insistence upon his own ideas ('a certain philosophy engendered in the whims of an Egotist') is reconciled with a sense of his peculiar and unique kind of greatness.

The last paragraph of Letter 93 contains the sentence 'I am ambitious of doing the world some good'. It is not the first time that Keats has sounded this note, for in Letter 62 we find the following:

I find that I can have no enjoyment in the World but continual drinking of Knowledge—I find there is no worthy pursuit but the idea of doing some good for the world—some do it with their society—some with their wit—some with their benevolence—some with a sort of power of conferring pleasure and good humour on all they meet and in a thousand ways all equally dutiful to the command of Great Nature—there is but one way for me—the road lies through application study and thought. I will pursue it and to that end purpose retiring for some years. I have been hovering for some time between an exquisite sense of the luxurious and a love for Philosophy—were I calculated for the former I should be glad—but as I am not I shall turn all my soul to the latter.

We may at first find it decidedly odd that Keats should say that he is *not* 'calculated' for 'an exquisite sense of the luxurious', but that he would be glad if he were. His predilection for 'the luxurious' evident in so much of the earlier poetry would seem to suggest the precise opposite, until we remember that by

24 April 1818, when Letter 62 was written, *Endymion* was finished and just about to be published. If Keats has not altogether left 'the luxurious' behind him, it will appear henceforward in contexts that do not sanction easy indulgence. 'To cease upon the midnight with no pain' may be a tempting thought, but the temptation is confronted and dismissed.

Whether or not 'Philosophy' would really and permanently have proved to be Keats's bent had be lived longer need not concern us. What does matter is that in Letter 93 he is still not satisfied with himself. The 'idea of doing some good for the world' returns, though this time it is not explicitly associated with 'application study and thought' in opposition to 'the luxurious':

In the second place I will speak of my views, and of the life I purpose to myself. I am ambitious of doing the world some good: if I should be spared that may be the work of maturer years—in the interval I will assay to reach to as high a summit in Poetry as the nerve bestowed upon me will suffer. The faint conceptions I have of Poems to come brings the blood frequently into my forehead.

The interesting point here is that although Keats does not speak of poetry in terms that are in any way contemptuous, he clearly does not suppose that it is precisely by writing poems that he stands the best chance of 'doing the world some good'! What follows, indeed, shows that if 'the luxurious' is no longer a temptation, Keats feels that poetry itself might conceivably become one: 'All I hope is that I may not lose all interest in human affairs—that the solitary indifference I feel for applause even from the finest Spirits, will not blunt any acuteness of vision I may have.' And even though he adds 'I do not think it will', the slight uneasiness is still there. Keats is conscious of a certain inclination in himself to ignore, even perhaps to scorn, whatever lies outside his preoccupations as a poetic artist; a dangerous tendency to rest in an attitude of self-sufficient isolation and aloofness. And he knows that this, if unchecked, must prove disastrous to his art, for an art which seeks arrogantly to detach itself from life can never be the great art that Keats aims to create.

But Keats, though aware of dangers, does not think that he will really succumb and thus lose his 'acuteness of vision': 'I feel assured that I should write from the mere yearning and fondness I have for the Beautiful even if my night's labours should be burnt every morning, and no eye ever shine upon them.' Read outside their context, the words 'yearning and fondness . . . for the Beautiful' might look suspiciously like the kind of narrow, precious utterance of one who has elevated Art and Beauty into the objects of a cult. Taken that way, they would not be at all inconsistent with loss of 'all interest in human affairs' and 'solitary indifference'. As it is, however, the context makes it plain that Keats's idea of 'the Beautiful', at this stage, includes and indeed depends upon the recognition that neither the artist nor his art can truly be regarded as self-sufficient, or 'superior' to the humanity from which, after all, they spring.

Letter 93 was written in October 1818; the following April Keats wrote the *Ode on a Grecian Urn*, in which the relations and differences between art and life are so subtly explored. The letter most commonly quoted in connection with that poem, however, is 31, which belongs to November 1817:

I am certain of nothing but of the holiness of the Heart's affections and the truth of Imagination—What the imagination seizes as Beauty must be truth—whether it existed before or not—for I have the same Idea of all our Passions as of Love they are all in their sublime, creative of essential Beauty.

The conclusion of the ode is so strikingly foreshadowed, in fact, that one is justifiably tempted to take this passage as offering the most completely satisfying gloss on 'Beauty is truth' that one could possibly wish for. No one, indeed, can doubt its relevance to the poem. In the light of Letter 31, the urn appears as both product and embodiment of the creative imagination. In other words, the exquisite work of art stands for the 'essential Beauty' brought into being by the imagination of the artist. So far there is nothing to question. But Keats insists in the letter that this beauty '*must be truth*—whether it existed before or not'. If that looks merely like a more clumsy way of saying 'Beauty is truth', we have to remember that those three words have a particular context in the poem, and are not, as we have already seen, an oracular utterance definitively stating the poet's own settled point of view. The fact is, that when Keats arrives at the stage of writing the ode, he can no longer accept his earlier statement that 'What the imagination seizes as Beauty must be truth' without qualification; and indeed one might well regard the entire ode as fundamentally a superbly organized way of qualifying those words. For the Keats of the ode, beauty and truth are more complicated matters than they are for the Keats of Letter 31.

But Letter 31 has other claims to fame. It contains the celebrated, even notorious exclamation, 'O, for a Life of Sensations rather than of Thoughts!' Once again we must be careful to place the words in their context:

The Imagination may be compared to Adam's dream—he awoke and found it truth. I am the more zealous in this affair, because I have never yet been able to perceive how any thing can be known for truth by consequitive reasoning—and yet it must be. Can it be that even the greatest Philosopher ever arrived at his goal without putting aside numerous objections. However it may be, O for a Life of Sensations rather than of Thoughts! It is 'a Vision in the form of Youth' a Shadow of reality to come—and this consideration has further convinced me for it has come as auxiliary to another favourite Speculation of mine, that we shall enjoy ourselves here after by having what we called happiness on Earth repeated in a finer tone and so repeated. And yet such a fate can only befall those who delight in Sensation rather than hunger as you do after Truth.

I call the exclamation 'notorious', because it is often quoted as evidence of a weakness in Keats—a namby-pamby, anti-intellectual addiction to the voluptuous. Some commentators, on the other hand, consider that the words should be taken far more seriously than that, that they point to what is most essential and valuable in Keats's genius, and that it is a good thing that he did *not* live long enough to find himself bogged down in the alien study of 'Philosophy'.

I do not see how we can help regarding the words as illustrating Keats's early predilection for 'the luxurious'. To take them more solemnly is to ignore the simple evidence of the early poems, not to mention later passages in the letters. Nor, I feel, can his speculation on life after death, his notion of the manner in which 'we shall enjoy ourselves here after', be viewed as anything more than callow whimsy. These things said, however, the fact remains that the words exist in a particular context; and that the context, while not inclining us to attach any great profundity to them, indicates that Keats was by no means so sure of their absolute rightness as the vigour of his exclamation would appear to suggest.

For one thing, Keats is not entirely happy about his attitude towards 'consequitive reasoning'. He may declare that he has 'never yet been able to perceive how any thing can be known for truth by consequitive reasoning', but he feels compelled to add '—and yet it must be'. The claims of 'consequitive reasoning', even though he does not yet understand them, cannot be easily brushed aside. Consider, moreover, what Keats has to say a little further on in the same letter:

I am continually running away from the subject—sure this cannot be exactly the case with a complex Mind—one that is imaginative and at the same time careful of its fruits—who would exist partly on Sensation partly on thought—to whom it is necessary that years should bring the philosophic mind—

This 'complex Mind', this idea of existing 'partly on Sensation partly on thought'—what are these things but a description of the Keats who was to write the odes and *The Fall of Hyperion*? Once we have realized this, we see that 'O for a Life of Sensations rather than of Thoughts!' is not taken completely seriously by Keats himself. The exclamation, though it reveals a youthful predilection, is not a statement of doctrine. It is rather a step in an exploratory discussion, a discussion initiated in Letter 31, and subsequently carried on within the poet himself, until the 'complex mind' was his own.

Letter 31, then, is a more mature utterance on the whole than its obvious inadequacies may lead us at first to suppose. So astoundingly rapid is Keats's development, indeed, that one cannot simply assume that the views expressed in a particular letter will be relatively immature merely because the letter is relatively early. No more vivid example of this can be found than

Letter 32, where we encounter what is perhaps his most valuable critical pronouncement:

I had not a dispute but a disquisition, with Dilke on various subjects; several things dove-tailed in my mind, and at once it struck me what quality went to form a Man of Achievement, especially in Literature, and which Shakespeare possessed so enormously—I mean *Negative Capability*, that is, when a man is capable of being in uncertainties, mysteries, doubts, without any irritable reaching after fact and reason—

Here Keats both adds a permanent critical term to the language, and tells us why his own *Fall of Hyperion* is a great poem.

INDEX OF PASSAGES QUOTED